On other works by Bob Avakian:

From Ike to Mao...and Beyond:

"Bob Avakian is a long distance runner in the freedom struggle against imperialism, racism and capitalism. His voice and witness are indispensable in our efforts to enhance the wretched of the earth. And his powerful story of commitment is timely."

Cornel West, Class of 1943 University Professor of Religion, Princeton University

"A truly interesting account of Bob Avakian's life, a humanizing portrait of someone who is often seen only as a hard-line revolutionary. I can understand why Bob Avakian has drawn so many ardent supporters. He speaks to people's alienation from a warlike and capitalist society, and holds out the possibility for radical change."

Howard Zinn, author of *A People's History of the United States*

"Berkeley-bred Avakian's new memoir, *From Ike to Mao and Beyond*, leaves a breathtaking impression. Having deepened and purified his convictions over 40 years of personal and political struggle. Avakian sounds a high, sustained cry for complete social transformation almost as if he were the trumpet of Lenin himself."

San Francisco Chronicle

"*From Ike To Mao and Beyond* is the memoir of a long distance runner whose disillusionment with imperialism, racism, and capitalism led him from his mainstream American background to embrace the ideals of revolutionary communism....A window into transparent injustice and one person's true-life determination to search for a better path, despite the scorn of the society around him."

The Midwest Book Review

"Bob Avakian brings candor and sometimes retrospective insight into what it means to grow up white and male in our patriarchal, capitalistic culture and still to emerge as a leader of the fight against social injustice. His memoir is fascinating and inspirational."

Carol Downer, Co-founder, Feminist Women's Heath Centers

Marxism and the Call of the Future (with Bill Martin)

"This brilliant, lively, and scholarly attempt to define communism's present role in addressing the need to remake our world is especially timely in the face of the policies and actions of the Bush administration. Bob Avakian and Bill Martin are to be commended for their steadfast endeavors to bring about a new society. We owe them both our gratitude for this monumental effort to move our world toward justice and righteousness."

Rev. George W. Webber, President Emeritus,
New York Theological Seminary

"...so important that it should stand on the shelf of everyone who cares about the destiny of the political Left...marks the beginning of a new approach."

Slavoj Žižek, author of *Iraq: The Borrowed Kettle* and *The Sublime Object of Ideology*

Revolution (DVD)

"Avakian...lucidly explains concepts ranging from dialectical materialism to irony without condescending to his audience... He's no less sharp when he's answering questions than when he's outlining his revolutionary program."

Jonathan Rosenbaum, *Chicago Reader*

"Recalling the vicious assaults on Claude Neal, Mary Turner and Emmett Till, Avakian provides a brutal and bloody outline of tragedy, and does it with a fervor that is far too uncommon coming from the mouth of a white man."

Herb Boyd, *Amsterdam News*

Preaching From a Pulpit of Bones:

"What is ethical thinking in a time of social fragmentation and imperialist globalization? Bob Avakian convincingly argues that morality has to be tied to a vision of a good society, a society free of exploitation and every form of domination. Even more does morality have to do with the struggle to create such a society. Avakian points the way toward what some doubt is possible, a materialist ethics. Like Mao's, this is a Marxism that aims at a social analysis that is clear and systematic but not 'cold'—a Marxism with heart."

Bill Martin, Associate Professor of Philosophy, DePaul University, Chicago, author of *Humanism and Its Aftermath*

Democracy: Can't We Do Better Than That?:

"Avakian argues his position on the decisive limitations of democracy in such a way that careful readers are compelled to clarify and rethink their own views. Avakian has written a serious and demanding work of political philosophy and political practice."

Norman K. Gottwald, editor of *The Bible and Liberation: Political and Social Hermeneutics*

"With marxist analysis Avakian takes apart the saints of liberal democratic theory: he guts Stuart Mill and shreds John Locke. To these ingredients he adds a dash of maoist seasoning—a *picante* dish!"

Ross Gandy, author of *Marx and History*

BOB AVAKIAN
•
OBSERVATIONS ON ART AND CULTURE, SCIENCE AND PHILOSOPHY

Insight Press, Inc.

Chicago

Grateful acknowledgment is made for permission to quote from the following:

The Demon-Haunted World: Science as a Candle in the Dark by Carl Sagan, Copyright © 1996 by Carl Sagan. Reprinted with permission from the Estate of Carl Sagan.

Science, Jews, and Secular Culture: Studies in Mid-Twentieth-Century American Intellectual History by David Hollinger, Copyright © 1998 by David Hollinger. Reprinted by permission.

FIRST EDITION

First Printing: July 2005
Second Printing: September 2005

Library of Congress Control Number: 2005930253

ISBN: 0-9760236-3-6

Contents

Publisher's Note

We are very happy to present this collection of reflections and observations by Bob Avakian on art, culture, science, and philosophy.

Excerpted from talks as well as more informal discussions and conversations, many of the texts in this collection invite the reader to experience the freewheeling Bob Avakian as he continues to develop his extensive body of work, with its many radical new directions, with regard to the communist project.

The observations collected here range from Avakian's reenvisioning of the dictatorship of the proletariat and his epistemological break-throughs in Marxism to reflections on truth and beauty, science and imagination, the problems of Lysenko-ism, and the relationship of Marxism to philosophy generally.

We believe this collection will provide the reader with important, fresh, and provocative insights and provoke further creative and critical thinking about the subjects discussed here.

Footnotes have been added for publication.

THE STRUGGLE IN THE REALM OF IDEAS[1]

I am going to talk for a while—I don't know how long, but usually the smart money bets that it'll be a little while. [*laughter*] And then we can have some questions and discussion. So I'm very excited about all this.

As you know, the title of this talk is "Dictatorship and Democracy, and the Socialist Transition to Communism," but before getting more directly into questions relating to that, I want to talk about the importance of working with ideas, and the struggle in the realm of ideas. Many of you have probably read the article on this subject which was printed in the *Revolutionary Worker* a while ago now by Ardea Skybreak, titled "Working with Ideas."[2] And the article stresses the importance of actually getting deeply into this realm in its own right, really wrangling with ideas, and having an open mind about what you're dealing with, and then ultimately taking your ideas into the real world, into the realm of practice, and testing them out there.

This is a very important approach generally for people in the sciences, or people generally who work in the realm of ideas. And it is something that people who seek to apply the outlook and methodology of communism should be the very best at. But that takes work. It isn't an automatic thing. Just because you take up the most scientific, the most comprehensive and systematic world outlook and method doesn't

---

1. This selection is excerpted from the talk *Dictatorship and Democracy, and the Socialist Transition to Communism,* the edited text of which is available online at revcom.us. This particular selection was published in *Revolutionary Worker* #1250 and #1251 (August 22 and August 29, 2004).

2. Ardea Skybreak, "Working with Ideas and Searching for Truth: A Reflection on Revolutionary Leadership and the Intellectual Process," *Revolutionary Worker* #1144 (March 24, 2002), available online at revcom.us.

mean that you are therefore automatically good at working with ideas, or that you automatically arrive at the truth about something. And conversely, as we have also emphasized, there are people who not only don't apply this outlook and method, but who disagree with it—or even detest it—who nevertheless discover important truths. And understanding that is also a very important part of really grasping and applying the world outlook and methodology of communism. That's the contradictory nature of it.

So working with ideas is a struggle in its own right. It's something that has to be gone into deeply in its own right, while of course ultimately it can't be divorced from the real world, from the world of practice, from people struggling to change the world, and from the masses of people in all the different endeavors and spheres of life that they engage in. But even while we keep that in mind and remain firmly grounded in that as a basic point of understanding and orientation, it's nonetheless crucial to recognize that in any sphere, if you are really going to learn about it and make changes in that sphere, you have to immerse yourself deeply in it, you have to engage other people who are also working in that sphere, and you have to take their ideas seriously.

One time someone wrote me a letter and asked: how do you read things, do you do what's called "proof-texting"?—which is a way of reading to refute something. Do you read it in order to make your point? What he was referring to was the approach of only looking for things that confirm what you already believe; for example, you start out with a disagreement with somebody and in reading what they write you look for those things that you don't agree with, things that prove your point, and then sort of tautologically you go around in a circle. You end up with: "Aha, it's wrong." And I replied, no I don't approach things that way. Even things I vehemently disagree with, going in, I still try to look to see what there is that they are grappling with, what ideas they may hit on even inadvertently or may stumble on, or may actually wrangle with more systematically. There are things to be learned even from reactionaries. There are things to learn from reactionaries, even about politics and ideology, let alone other spheres. That doesn't mean we take up their outlook or their politics. [laughs] But there are things to be learned. And this is an important point of orientation.

Now, I'm stressing this because, on the one hand, we know that the backbone of the revolution will be the masses of exploited and oppressed proletarians; but there is a great importance to winning people, and to bringing forward people broadly, from among other strata.

And in particular there is an importance to bringing forward people from among the intelligentsia—winning them to sympathy and support for our project and our vision of a radically different world, a communist world. We need to increasingly win as many of them as possible to become revolutionary communist intellectuals, actively partisan to our cause, and more than that, to become part of the vanguard. There can never be a communist revolution without this.

And there is a real question that comes up and is often raised: Can you actually work with ideas in a critical and creative way and be a member of a vanguard communist party? Or can you really do creative work in the arts or sciences and be a member of such a party? Many people answer this by adamantly saying no—that, by definition, a party that is disciplined, that applies democratic centralism, that has a strong central core of leadership, and in some cases has a very strong individual leader, by definition will stifle the initiative of other people, will prevent them from really thinking creatively and critically, and will prevent them from bringing forward anything new; that by the dint and weight of the discipline and "bureaucracy" of such an organization, it's bound to crush and suffocate any kind of creative and critical impulse.

Well [laughs], this is a real question, and it doesn't have an easy answer. I do believe that fundamentally the answer is and must be resoundingly yes, this can be done. But again, it's not easy, and it's not simple and we haven't entirely solved this problem in the history of the international communist movement. There is much more to be learned, critically summed up and brought forward, that is new in this regard. There is important experience of the international communist movement and socialist society and the dictatorship of the proletariat, very real positive experience in this sphere, but also considerable negative experience, which again, needs to be critically examined and deeply and all-sidedly summed up. And, frankly, we need to learn how to do a lot better.

For example, I have spoken a number of times in various writings and talks about the Lysenko experience in the Soviet Union.[3] Lysenko was an agronomist, a botanist, who claimed to have brought forward new strains of wheat that would make production leap ahead in agri-

---

3. See "The Proletariat and the Bourgeoisie...Soaring to Great Heights...and Grubbing in the Dirt," *Revolutionary Worker* #1086 (January 14, 2001); "Once Again on the Intellectuals," *Revolutionary Worker* #1087 (January 21, 2001); and "We Can't Know Everything—So We Should Be Good at Learning," in this volume. All of these articles are available online at revcom.us.

culture. And this was a real problem in the Soviet Union, that agriculture was seriously lagging industry. And, of course, if that gap continues to widen it throws the whole economy out of whack and basically unhinges your attempts to build a socialist economy. So this was a very severe problem they were facing, particularly in the early and mid-1930s. And Lysenko basically brought forward a theory which contradicted basic principles of evolution and fell into the whole idea of the inheritability of acquired characteristics and so on, which is not scientifically correct. But pragmatically it seemed like a way to solve the agricultural problems, so Stalin and others threw a lot of weight behind Lysenko. And this did a lot of damage. Not only in the short run and in a more narrow sense—it didn't lead to the results that they were hoping for—but it also did a lot of damage in the broader sense in terms of how people were being trained to think, and how they were being trained to handle the relationship between theory and practice, and reality and understanding and transforming reality. There's a way in which this has had long-term negative consequences. First of all, it did in the Soviet Union. And it did in the international communist movement, because it trained people to think in a certain erroneous way.

Now, this situation was very complicated, because many of the people who were the experts and authorities in the field of biology, botany, and so on in the Soviet Union were carried forward from the old society. And many of them were political and ideological reactionaries. So here you see the contradiction is very acutely posed. Lysenko was trying to make a breakthrough to advance the socialist cause, and being opposed by authorities, many of whom—not all, but many of whom—were political and ideological reactionaries. But it just so happened that they were more correct than him about the basic point at issue. Yet political expediency dictated what was done there, and the people who were critical were actually suppressed.

So you can see the complexity of the problem. And it's not so easy to handle. These are real life-and-death questions. Whether people eat is a life-and-death question. That's what was at issue, was whether people eat, whether they have clothes in the winter. And the Russian winter is worse than Chicago, okay?

When you have a socialist economy you are not relying on the imperialists any more. And you are not relying on exploiting the masses of people. So you are trying to bring forward new forms, new relations in which to carry out production, and "it's all on you"—it's all on us, it's on the proletariat, it's on its vanguard, it's on the masses of people. How do you solve these problems?

Well, Lysenko was trying to solve this problem, but the method he came up with wasn't correct. But what was worse, was that he was supported out of instrumentalist thinking. In other words, you make your ideas an instrument of your desires or aims. You want something to happen, so you "reconstruct reality" so it falls in line with what you want. You make reality an instrument of predetermined aims, rather than proceeding from what reality actually is, and then figuring out how to transform it on the basis of what it actually is and how it's actually moving and changing and developing, which reality always is. So this is a fundamental question of outlook and methodology.

And, beyond this particular experience of Lysenko, there is overall a real contradiction and real tension that objectively exists between the line and discipline of a party at any given time, and creative, critical thinking and work in the realm of ideas broadly speaking. There is a real, objective tension. The party is trying to mobilize its own ranks and the masses to change reality. It has to make its best estimate of what the key aspects of reality are at any given time, and how to go about mobilizing people to change them. Which means by definition that there are many things that it can't pay attention to at any given time. And we have to resist the tendency to "know-it-all-ism." Communists are people who by definition have strong convictions [*laughs*]. So, there's nothing that goes on that communists don't have an opinion about. [*laughter*] But it is very important to know the difference between your opinion and what's well-established, scientific fact, that has been determined and established from many different directions through a whole process to be the best approximation you can make of reality at a given time. You go into a movie, you have an opinion coming out. But your opinion is just that. And it's very important, especially for communists, and especially for leaders of a communist movement and a communist party, to know the difference between their impressions and opinions and what is scientifically grounded fact that is established through many different pathways, has been deeply and all-sidedly confirmed to be true.

So this is another contradiction we have to deal with. You are trying to change reality, and you are trying to grasp reality in its changingness, so to speak—because it doesn't stand still and wait for you to understand it, it's moving, changing—and you are trying to mobilize people to grasp and to change reality. And you have to all pull together to do that. In a real vanguard party you can't have people all going off in different directions, all implementing their own lines, and still mobilize masses of people to change reality. But by definition when you do that—when you all pull together to mobilize masses of people—there is a danger and a tendency to impose thinking from the top. It would be simple if it were just a bureaucratic problem, but there is a necessity to mobilize people behind what you understand to be true, and that does require leadership and, many times, mobilizing people "from the top."

How do you handle that contradiction—between mobilizing people around what you understand to be true, while at the same time having a critical attitude and being open to the understanding that you may not be right about this or that particular, or even about big questions? That's a very difficult contradiction to handle correctly. It's something we have to sum up and learn how to do better on as well. And it's not easy. But we do have to do better.

The essence of the problem is not, as people sometimes say, learning to think for yourself. In something I wrote a number of years ago, I pointed out that, on the one hand, this is kind of a truism, thinking for yourself. It's impossible to think with anybody else's brain. [*laughter*] So, in one way or another you are always thinking for yourself. You are always using your own mind to think. The question more essentially is, are you thinking according to one outlook and methodology or another. That's the fundamental question that's involved. It's not "free thinking" in the abstract, or as some principle raised above everything else, but thinking in accordance with and by applying the outlook and methodology of communism in order to arrive, in the most comprehensive and systematic way, at an understanding of reality. Not all of reality—that's never possible—but the essential things that you can identify at a given time that you need to deeply go into, understand and transform, while having an open mind about both those things you're not paying attention to, and even those things you are. And you have to do this even while you are moving forward to change these things.

So the essence is not free thinking, but what outlook and methodology you are thinking with. But there is an element of free thinking that has to be involved. And this should certainly be no less true for communists than for other people. It should be more true. And that's where you do run into contradiction and tension. Because free thinking in a communist party—a disciplined, democratic centralist party—doesn't come automatically and spontaneously either. Or if it does, it often goes off in directions that are harmful. How to get that right, how to handle that contradiction correctly, is something we need to do more work on.

All that I have been speaking to so far has a lot to do with a principle that Mao emphasized—that Marxism embraces but does not replace all these different spheres of society and human endeavor. Each of them has their own, as Mao put it, particularity of contradiction. Each of them has its own particular features. Each of them has things that have to be dug into deeply and wrestled with and wrangled with in an all-sided and deep-going way. That was the point of that Ardea Skybreak article. And whether it's music, or physics, or biology, or any sphere that you can think of, there are particularities to these things that people who are in these fields are grappling with all the time.

In the history of the Chinese revolution, and in particular through the Cultural Revolution, they brought forward the principle of red and expert, with red leading expert. In other words, the communists and communist line should lead experts in various fields. Which is an important principle because otherwise other ideologies are in command, and they are leading away from the ability to actually synthesize correctly all that people are engaging and learning about, even to arrive most deeply at the truth about a particular sphere.

So this is an important principle—combining red and expert, and red leading expert—but if you are going to lead in a sphere, the first thing you have to do is be good at learning. And you have to be good at drawing forward those people who are in that field who are also advanced ideologically and politically. People like that are a very important lever and link. Now, as Mao said, if you go to the opera—which is a popular form in China—if you go to the opera long enough you can become an expert, even if you can't sing or compose at all. But to be able to comprehensively understand something requires really being immersed in it.

This relates to one of the big divisions in society that we have: the "mental/manual contradiction," as we call it for short. Masses of people are locked out not only of particular fields of knowledge, but are locked out of the chance to grapple with the whole sphere of working with ideas. Now, there are exceptions. Everybody knows exceptions. People who go to prison, in the most horrific conditions, who become very developed intellectuals. Some of them become revolutionary intellectuals and even communists. But those are the exceptions, because the conditions are working overwhelmingly against that. Just think about the masses of people and the conditions that people have to work in and the conditions that kids grow up in. Where do they develop the ability to work with ideas? It's suffocated out of them, it's squeezed out of them, from a very early age.

This is one of the big contradictions that we have to overcome through the whole transition to communism. Because, as long as this contradiction exists, there is always the basis for it to turn into a relationship of oppression and exploitation. To run a society, you have to work with ideas, you have to think. There's no way around it. You can't just do it by taking revenge on the people who used to rule it. That may bring very momentary satisfaction for some. But it's not what this is about, and it doesn't lead to the kind of transformations we need. You have to think. You have to work with ideas. But on the other hand, you have to do it without reinforcing, and in fact overcoming, this great divide, between a small number of people, relatively speaking, in the world who have been able to really get into this whole sphere of "working with ideas," and on the other hand the masses of people who have been essentially locked out of this.

Remember that movie *Contact*, I think it was called. It was based on the Carl Sagan thing about contact with people from outer space, and Jodie Foster was in it. And there is this character played by Matthew McConaughey who at one point says to her, basically: "What makes you such a smart-ass? 95% of the people of the world believe in religion. And you don't. What makes you think you know something that they don't?" Well that's the contradiction. Because, the "5%" of the people (it's actually more than that) who don't believe in religion are right. But the masses of people don't have the ability to come to the conclusions that this minority of people has come to, because the masses are not only locked out of certain knowledge, they're locked out of learning how to work with ideas and wrangle in this whole realm.

So this is one of the big things we have to overcome, and we can't do it by crude methods. We have to do it by applying some of the principles that Mao emphasized, including the principle of "embraces but does not replace."[4] We have to do it by learning how to work with and learn from and synthesize what people in these spheres are bringing forward, and then win them over, particularly the advanced, to that synthesis, and unite with them to win and influence the broader ranks of people, while continuing to learn from them.

---

4. See "Marxism 'Embraces But Does Not Replace'," in this volume. Available online at revcom.us.

This is one of those tricky things. There is a lot of resentment among masses against the intellectuals. In China, for example, the Mandarins, the people who were the educated classes, really lorded it over the masses of people. They grew long fingernails just to make the point that they didn't have to do manual labor. This was a sign of distinction. "I'm not in that class. You carry my luggage. I don't do that kind of thing." Well, in this society you don't have that. But you do have great gaps. And there is, on the one hand, looking down on people and, on the other hand, a lot of resentment. And we have to overcome that from both sides. People have to understand the role and the importance of theory and working with ideas. We have to bring forward those among the masses who have more ability to do that at any given time, not because they are superior to the others, but just because through a lot of accident and particular circumstances they've been able to develop some ability to do that. And we have to use them as levers and links—I don't mean use them in a narrow, utilitarian sense of using people—I mean unleash them to be levers and links to bring forward broader masses of people.

When people come forward from among the masses who develop the ability to work with ideas and to take up theory, it's important that they work in that sphere in its own right on the one hand, but also that they be a lever and link to broader masses of people, to help break some of this down for the masses of people and show them that it's not a mystery, and help them begin to take up some of these questions themselves.

And that's not easy. We've had experience which has driven home that it is not so easy. We used to think, when we first started out, well, you bring forward people who come from among the masses, and naturally they will be able to go talk to other people about all these questions. But there's another leap involved there. You are not the same as you were. You are not the same anymore and you are not the same as the other masses, and they don't see things the way you do. So it's not so easy. It requires leadership and work to take another leap to where you really grasp it deeply enough that you can break it back down to people and open the door to them to begin to grapple with these ideas.

We won't be able to do this on a massive scale until we have state power. This mental/manual division cannot be broken down in this society, but we can make advances toward it. And we should never accept it in principle, or bow down to it in any kind of strategic sense. But it's another reason why we need revolution. We cannot overcome this within the confines of this society. This society will continue to reinforce these divisions, even as we are working against them. All of this has to be part of a revolutionary movement to overthrow this system and to bring into being a new society where then we can really go after these contradictions and overcome them in the correct way. Not in a narrow philistine way, where we denigrate and downgrade and look down upon work in the realm of ideas, but where we appreciate it fully and yet bring the masses into it fully in the correct way. It's a very complex and arduous, long-term struggle to achieve that. And it's one of the most important aspects of advancing ultimately to communism.

So that's by way of background to the main points I want to get into.

And I want to say that, in light of all this, it is crucial that we ourselves develop and deepen our own grasp of first of all the importance of working with ideas and the struggle in this whole realm, and of the correct orientation and method for approaching work in relation to this, which has to do with for whom and for what this is all for, and has to do with what outlook and methodology you bring in working and struggling in the realm of ideas.

Now, certainly not the only, but one of the most important focuses of this at this time is the struggle to confront and combat the constant attacks on the experience of socialist countries, and in particular of the dictatorship of the proletariat, and especially the whole concept of totalitarianism; and at the same time, while doing that, to confront and critically examine the actual experience of socialist countries and the dictatorship of the proletariat, drawing the fullest lessons from this experience—mainly and overwhelmingly the positive lessons, but also facing squarely and digging deeply into the very real shortcomings and errors.

I was reading an interesting comment from someone—it was actually someone in the international movement—and they made the point, "I uphold very firmly the experience of the socialist revolution so far, but I don't want to live in those countries" [*laughter*]. In other words, we have a lot of work to do, to do better the next time around. That's a very dialectical attitude. And a materialist attitude: we should uphold these things historically, there are great achievements; but we also have to build on it and go farther and do better in certain areas, or else people won't want to live in these societies—and probably we won't either.

So we do have to confront and combat these attacks, while at the same time squarely confronting and digging deeply into the very real shortcomings and errors. There is a real and very urgent and pressing need to refute the attacks on socialism and the dictatorship of the proletariat, in a thoroughgoing, deep and living way—not a dogmatic way or stereotypical way. This is a crucial focus of the class struggle right now in the ideological realm. And how well we carry out this struggle has profound implications for work that's guided and inspired by the strategic objectives of revolution, socialism, and ultimately a communist world.

This applies broadly, and it has important application among the proletariat and basic masses. First of all, it's a real mistake to think that these questions don't find their way among the masses. You know, the people have heard this, they've heard that. It doesn't mean they've read long dissertations or analyses, but they've heard this and they've heard that, and it has seeped down into the popular consciousness, and it's pumped at them all the time in various ways. These summations that are blared out, and sometimes elaborated on in intellectual theses, are also very simply boiled down and blasted at the masses all the time. Plus, they have some real questions that they come up against when thinking about whether the world could be different. There is not just propaganda from the bourgeoisie that raises questions in their mind, but real contradictions in life that they are wrangling with and legitimately want answers to. And we have to not only give them answers, but again, we have to draw them into the process of finding the answers. But there is work to be done by people who do have a more advanced understanding and a developed ability, or developing ability, to work with ideas, to grapple in this realm.

There is importance to combating these attacks on communism and to digging into these questions deeply among the proletariat, among the basic masses of people in society. But there also is particular and particularly important application of this in relation to the intelligentsia. And this goes back to what I was saying at the beginning.

THREE ALTERNATIVE WORLDS [1]

As the world exists today and as people seek to change it, and particularly in terms of the socialist transformation of society, as I see it there are basically three alternatives that are possible. One is the world as it is. Enough said about that. [*Laughter.*]

The second one is in a certain sense, almost literally and mechanically, turning the world upside down. In other words, people who are now exploited will no longer be exploited in the same way, people who now rule this society will be prevented from ruling or influencing society in a significant way. The basic economic structure of society will change, some of the social relations will change, and some of the forms of political rule will change, and some of the forms of culture and ideology will change, but fundamentally the masses of people will not be increasingly and in one leap after another drawn into the process of really transforming society. This is really a vision of a revisionist society. If you think back to the days of the Soviet Union, when it had become a revisionist society, capitalist and imperialist in essence, but still socialist in name, when they would be chided for their alleged or real violations of people's rights, they would often answer "Who are you in the West to be talking about the violation of human rights—look at all the people in your society who are unemployed, what more basic human right is there than to have a job?"

Well, did they have a point? Yes, up to a point. But fundamentally what they were putting forward, the vision of society that they were projecting, was a social welfare kind of society in which fundamentally

---

1. This selection is excerpted from the talk *Dictatorship and Democracy, and the Socialist Transition to Communism,* the edited text of which is available online at revcom.us. This particular selection was published in *Revolutionary Worker* #1257 (October 31, 2004).

the role of the masses of people is no different than it is under the classical form of capitalism. The answer about the rights of the people cannot be reduced to the right to have a job and earn an income, as basic as that is. There is the question of are we really going to transform society so that in every respect, not only economically but socially, politically, ideologically, and culturally, it really is superior to capitalist society. A society that not only meets the needs of the masses of people, but really is characterized increasingly by the conscious expression and initiative of the masses of people.

This is a more fundamental transformation than simply a kind of social welfare, socialist in name but really capitalist in essence society, where the role of the masses of people is still largely reduced to being producers of wealth, but not people who thrash out all the larger questions of affairs of state, the direction of society, culture, philosophy, science, the arts, and so on. The revisionist model is a narrow, economist view of socialism. It reduces the people, in their activity, to simply the economic sphere of society, and in a limited way at that—simply their social welfare with regard to the economy. It doesn't even think about transforming the world outlook of the people as they in turn change the world around them.

And you cannot have a new society and a new world with the same outlook that people are indoctrinated and inculcated with in this society. You cannot have a real revolutionary transformation of society and abolition of unequal social as well as economic relations and political relations if people still approach the world in the way in which they're conditioned and limited and constrained to approach it now. How can the masses of people really take up the task of consciously changing the world if their outlook and their approach to the world remains what it is under this system? It's impossible, and this situation will simply reproduce the great inequalities in every sphere of society that I've been talking about.

The third alternative is a real radical rupture. Marx and Engels said in the *Communist Manifesto* that the communist revolution represents a radical rupture with traditional property relations and with traditional ideas. And the one is not possible without the other. They are mutually reinforcing, one way or the other.

If you have a society in which the fundamental role of women is to be breeders of children, how can you have a society in which there is equality between men and women? You cannot. And if you don't attack and uproot the traditions, the morals, and so on, that reinforce that role, how can you transform the relations between men and women and abolish the deep-seated inequalities that are bound up with the whole division of society into oppressors and oppressed, exploiters and exploited? You cannot.

So the third alternative is a real radical rupture in every sphere, a radically different synthesis, to put it that way. Or to put it another way, it's a society and a world that the great majority of people would actually want to live in. One in which not only do they not have to worry about where their next meal is coming from, or if they get sick whether they're going to be told that they can't have health care because they can't pay for it, as important as that is; but one in which they are actually taking up, wrangling with, and increasingly making their own province all the different spheres of society.

Achieving that kind of a society, and that kind of a world, is a very profound challenge. It's much more profound than simply changing a few forms of ownership of the economy and making sure that, on that basis, people's social welfare is taken care of, but you still have people who are taking care of that *for* the masses of people; and all the spheres of science, the arts, philosophy and all the rest are basically the province of a few. And the political decision-making process remains the province of a few.

To really leap beyond that is a tremendous and world-historic struggle that we've been embarked on since the Russian revolution (not counting the very short-lived and limited experience of the Paris Commune)—and in which we reached the high point with the Chinese revolution and in particular the Cultural Revolution—but from which we've been thrown back temporarily.

So we need to make a further leap on the basis of summing up very deeply all that experience. There are some very real and vexing problems that we have to confront and advance through in order to draw from the best of the past, but go further and do even better in the future.

Now I want to say a few things in this context about totalitarianism. Just as an aside here, I find it very interesting that you can read innumerable books delving deeply into the psyche of Stalin or Lenin or Mao—"What went on in the deranged minds of these people [*laughter*] that led them to think they could remake the world in their maddened image [*laughter*] and led them, in the name of some greater moral good, to bring great catastrophe on the humanity that they were affecting?" I don't know how many books I've seen like that. I have never yet seen—

maybe there are some, but I have never seen—a study of the deranged psyche of Thomas Jefferson [*laughter*] or George Washington: "How is it that a person could come to believe in their own mind [*laughter*] that they were benefiting not only humanity in general, but other human beings whom they owned? [*laughter*] What depth of psychological derangement must be involved in that? [*laughter*]. What is more totalitarian than actually owning other human beings?"

Or what about the study of the depths of the depraved minds of Lyndon Johnson or Ronald Reagan [*laughter*], who murdered millions of people, including vast numbers of children? "What must have gone wrong, somewhere in their childhood or somewhere else in their lives? [*laughter*] What demented ideas must they somehow have internalized that led them to believe that in the name of the shining city on the hill, or whatever [*laughter*], they had the right and the obligation to slaughter thousands and millions of innocent people?"

I have never seen those studies. Certainly I haven't read about them in the *New York Times Book Review* section. [*laughter*]

Still, there are some real questions that are raised about totalitarianism by the ideologues and the "intellectual camp followers" of the imperialists that do need to be taken on. In particular, they make the charge that in a society which they call totalitarian, but which is in reality the dictatorship of the proletariat, there is first of all an official ideology that everyone has to profess belief in, in order to get along in that society. And there is an official politics that everyone has to be involved in, in order to get along in that society and not get in trouble. Well, what about this?

Fundamentally, this is a distortion of what has gone on in socialist societies: why these revolutions were necessary in the first place and what they were seeking to accomplish and to overcome, and how they were going about doing that. The reality is that, for the great masses of people in capitalist (and certainly in feudal) society, they are barred from really being involved in any significant way in official politics and the politics that actually affect the affairs of state and the direction of society. And they are indoctrinated with an outlook and methodology and ideology that prevents them—discourages them and actively obstructs them—from really understanding the world as it is and changing it consciously. And that is what socialist revolutions seek to change, as well as bringing about fundamental changes in the economy and the social relations.

But what about this question of official ideology that everyone has to profess? Well, I think we have more to sum up about that from the history of socialist society and the dictatorship of the proletariat so far.

With regard to the question of the party, I think two things are definitely true. One, you need a vanguard party to lead this revolution and to lead the new state. Two, that party has to have an ideology that unifies it, an ideology that correctly reflects and enables people to consciously change reality, which is communist ideology.

But, more broadly, should everyone in society have to profess this ideology in order to get along? No. Those who are won over to this ideology should proclaim it and struggle for it. Those who are not convinced of it should say so. Those who disagree with it should say that. And there should be struggle. Something has to lead—the correct ideology that really enables people to get at the truth, and to do something with it in their interests, has to lead; but that doesn't mean everyone should have to profess it, in my opinion. And this is just my opinion. But it's worth digging into this a bit, it's worth exploring and wrangling with the question.

THE ROLE OF DISSENT IN A VIBRANT SOCIETY [1]

Socialist society should be a very lively and vibrant society, full of wrangling and struggle over all kinds of questions, in which we're moving step by step narrow and finally to eliminate the differences and inequalities that mean that some people are locked out of whole spheres of society. But that's a process that's going to go through stages, and through twists and turns, and not in a straight upward line. And at each stage there will be a very acute contradiction between holding onto power and continuing on the socialist road while at the same time drawing ever greater numbers of masses of people into this process, overcoming these inequalities to the greatest degree possible at every stage, and laying the basis to make further leaps in the future with regard to things that you cannot overcome at the present time.

The challenge is one of developing and applying the correct principles and methods so that all of this develops in such a way that it serves the advance toward communism, toward a communist world, so that socialist society is a vital and vibrant society in which masses of people are, in a great diversity of ways, increasingly wrangling with and engaging all kinds of questions having to do with the nature and direction of society; and, through all this, not only is political power maintained in a way that serves the fundamental interests and needs of the masses of the people and the world revolution, but the advance is carried forward toward the eventual abolition of state power altogether and the emergence of a community of freely associating human beings all over the world, a communist world where, to quote Mao, human

---

1. This selection is excerpted from the talk *Dictatorship and Democracy, and the Socialist Transition to Communism,* the edited text of which is available online at revcom.us. This particular selection was published in *Revolutionary Worker* #1257 and 1258 (October 31 and November 14, 2004).

beings consciously and voluntarily transform themselves and the objective world. And all this will be achieved through a wrenching process of struggle and wrangling, and not in some orderly, neat straightline way, and not with uniformity of opinion about everything all the time, by any means.

So democracy under the dictatorship of the proletariat, democracy for the vast masses of people, has to take in all these dimensions. It doesn't just mean that they have the right to speak out freely without being suppressed—which it does mean and must mean—but it means much more than that. It means not only their ability to associate politically and to demonstrate and to criticize, to raise disagreements with the official policy at any given time, or even with the leading ideology at any given time. But it also means that this has to be done in such a way that it's moving toward the withering away, first of all of dictatorship—that is, rule in society by one class over another and its use of an apparatus of repression, that is, armed forces, police, courts, and so on, to enforce its rule and to suppress those who would seek to overthrow it. Not only do we have to be moving toward the eventual withering away of all this and developing and applying concrete steps which actually lead to that—not just mouthing the words that we're working toward this withering away, but actually developing concrete forms and institutions that lead in that direction. But, together with that, we also have to be moving toward the withering away of democracy.

That, of course, is a very controversial statement. What do I mean by that? What I mean is *not* that through the advance of the dictatorship of the proletariat there is less and less democracy for the masses of people, until eventually it's eliminated altogether! That's not what we mean by the withering away of democracy together with the withering away of dictatorship. What we mean is, in essence, the opposite of that. We mean that the forms and means are developed through which the masses of people, in a certain sense, "naturally" take up, wrangle with, and ultimately make decisions about all different spheres of society.

As I spoke to in a series that was printed in the *RW*—excerpts from a talk I gave, *Getting Over the Two Great Humps*[2]—it means that

---

2. *Getting Over the Two Great Humps: Further Thoughts on Conquering the World* is a talk given by Bob Avakian in the late 1990s. Excerpts from this talk appeared in the *Revolutionary Worker* and are available online at revcom.us. The series "On Proletarian Democracy and Proletarian Dictatorship – A Radically Different View of Leading Society" appeared in *RW* #1214 through 1226 (October 5, 2003-January 25, 2004). The series "Getting Over the Hump" appeared in *RW* #927, 930, 932, and

the institutions and structures that are necessary to ensure that the rights of the people are upheld, and that one part of society, even among the people, is not being suppressed by another part—those structures and institutions no longer are necessary, and new structures and institutions are brought into being which correspond to and give expression to the fact that among the people there are no exploiters and exploited, there are no profound social divisions that lead to exploiters and exploited. At that point it will no longer be a question in society about whether one group among the people is going to oppress and dominate another. We will have moved, both in material reality and in the thinking of the people, beyond the point where that is even a possibility, because the economic and social conditions have been brought into being and, together with them, the political structures and institutions and political processes, and the ways of thinking and the culture have developed in such a way that the idea of one person, or one group in society, exploiting and oppressing another will be understood to be outrageous, absurd—and impossible.

Marx said about the future world, the world of communism, that it will seem as ridiculous and outrageous for one part of society to privately own the land, and everything that goes along with that, as it now seems for one human being to own another. Communism will mean that we have reached the point where the very idea that the way society should advance is for a few to benefit and then to proclaim that to be in the general interest of the society, where that idea will seem so ridiculous and outrageous that in a certain sense, to put it simply, it couldn't get a hearing. Where people would investigate what is the problem mentally [laughter]—what chemical imbalance has caused someone to talk in this way. [laughter]

Now we have to be careful, because dissent and people disagreeing with the established norm is always going to have to fight an uphill fight. This will undoubtedly be true in communist society as well. As Mao put it, newly emerging truths are always in the hands of a minority. So even under communism that will be true. The point is that there won't be organs of political suppression, so that if you bring forward unpopular ideas or new and different proposals for how things ought to

---

936-940 (October 12, November 2, November 16, and December 14, 1997 through January 18, 1998). Two additional excerpts from this talk are "Materialism and Romanticism: Can We Do Without Myth" in *RW* #1211 (August 24, 2003) and "Rereading George Jackson" in *RW* #968 (August 9, 1998). All of these excerpts can be found online at revcom.us.

be, people might think you are odd, but you are not going to become the object of political suppression or of social suppression, even without a state.

You can see why this requires not only transformation of material, economic, and social conditions, but also the thinking of the people. Even the slogan "from each according to their ability to each according to their needs" would never work under the present ideological conditions we have. What are my needs—well, you know, I need some new rims for my car. You could just go on, and the whole thing will come flying apart. This requires an ideological transformation where people see needs very differently. Needs are socially conditioned in any case. The idea that you need rims for your wheels is socially conditioned. That's not something that you thought of all on your own, in a vacuum. So, as you transform the material conditions, you transform the thinking of the people—so that individuals are thinking about their needs in relation to the larger interests of society, and are "naturally" subordinating their own individual interests to the larger interests of society, while still not obliterating the role and the needs of individuals and individuality. That requires a major ideological transformation. That's part of what has to go on too, in order to advance to communism.

Now, another aspect of this that I want to speak to briefly is what I call "the synthesis of the points that were emphasized in the polemic against K. Venu and some arguments made by John Stuart Mill." Now, in this polemic against K. Venu[3] I basically made the point that we can't have bourgeois democracy, we have to have the dictatorship of the proletariat. If we try to implement all these instrumentalities of mass democracy without any distinction among the people, we are going to hand power back over to the bourgeoisie, after everything people have gone through to seize power in the first place and all the sacrifice that that has required. In socialist society, we still have to have a vanguard party that leads, and we have to have an ideology that leads. Even if we don't want to insist that everybody has to profess that ideology whether they agree with it or not, we still have to have a vanguard party that leads, and an ideology that leads. This is one of the points that I was stressing in that polemic. But what I am referring to by synthesizing that, combining it in the correct way, with arguments of John Stuart

---

3. Avakian, "Democracy, More Than Ever We Can and Must Do Better Than That," appendix to *Phony Communism Is Dead...Long Live Real Communism!*, 2nd edition (Chicago: RCP Publications, 2004).

Mill is that Mill makes the argument that no opinion should be discounted, let alone suppressed in society, until all those people who wish to argue for it have had an opportunity to do so. And he goes on further to make the point that it is not enough to hear ideas characterized by those who oppose them, it is necessary to hear them put forward by people who are ardent advocates of those ideas—in the book *Democracy: Can't We Do Better Than That?*[4] I addressed this.

Well, of course, as I spoke to earlier, what he argues for can never literally be implemented. There is always somebody who wants to make one more argument for an idea.[*laughs*] There does come a time when you have to close the debate, at least for the time being. There are material reasons underlying that, and there are also reasons of politics. Decisions have to get made at certain points. You can't just go on arguing endlessly and conducting searches to see if there is anybody else who wants to argue for a point of view that nobody else agrees with.

Still, there is a point that Mill is getting at with this argument that it's not enough to hear positions characterized by those who oppose them, it is necessary to hear ardent advocates arguing for these positions. This relates to something that I think we have to incorporate more into the dictatorship of the proletariat and the rule and transformation of society by the masses of people. And this goes along with not just tolerating but encouraging dissent: we have to allow for people to explore many different ideas, and to hear advocates of many different ideas—without giving up the whole game, without losing power, without undermining and destroying the dictatorship of the proletariat. And that, once again, is a very complex and acute contradiction.

In order to handle this correctly, there are a couple of principles that I think are very important. One was actually articulated for me in a conversation that I had not long ago with a spoken word artist and poet. I was laying out to him how I saw socialist society and some of the same points that I'm making here about how we have to hang onto power and keep things going in a forward direction toward communism, while on the other hand there is a need for a lot of experimentation in the arts, a lot of critical thinking that needs to go on in the sciences and all these different spheres, and you have to let people take the ball and run with it, and not supervise them at every point on everything they do. And I asked him, for example: could you write your

---

4. Bob Avakian, *Democracy: Can't We Do Better Than That?* (Chicago: Banner Press, 1986).

poetry if every step of the way there was a party cadre there looking over your shoulder, examining what you are writing? He said "no way."

Then, as we discussed this for a while, he came up with what I thought was a very good formulation. He said, "It sounds to me like what you are talking about is 'a solid core with a lot of elasticity.'" And I said "yeah, you've really hit on something there," because that was exactly what I was trying to give voice to—that you have to have a solid core that firmly grasps and is committed to the strategic objectives and aims and process of the struggle for communism. If you let go of that you are just giving everything back to the capitalists in one form or another, with all the horrors that means. At the same time, if you don't allow for a lot of diversity and people running in all kinds of directions with things, then not only are people going to be building up tremendous resentment against you, but you are also not going to have the rich kind of process out of which the greatest truth and ability to transform reality will emerge.

So this is another expression of a very difficult contradiction that we have to learn how to handle a lot better. Mao had some good ideas about this, and struggled a lot to get the party to implement them. Mao was wrangling with this, but he was only able to get so far with it. As he pointed out, human life is finite. He was only able to get so far with it, and then he died and what happened in China happened. And people—in particular the people now ruling that society—no longer were concerned with wrangling with that contradiction.

So we have to take this up and go further and learn to do even better with it the next time around. And in order for that to happen, those who are won to or seriously grappling with the question of this whole revolutionary process have to start engaging these questions now, and prepare ourselves as well as bring forward broader and broader ranks of the masses to be wrangling with these things, so that when we do seize power here and there, we are further along in our ability to be dealing with these things in a much more practical sense, even while, as I said, continuing to wrangle with them in the realm of theory.

Now what goes along with the principle of "solid core with a lot of elasticity" is another very important principle and method, which I characterize this way: being able to distinguish the difference between those times and circumstances where it is really necessary to hold the reins tightly, and pay very detailed attention to things, on the one hand; and, on the other hand, those times and circumstances where it is not necessary to do this, and in fact it is much better not to do so. And if you think about it, this contradiction applies to all kinds of things on all kinds of levels. In anything that you take up at any given time, there are always aspects that, if you don't pay great detailed attention to them, and even in certain ways insist that "this is the way this has to be done," the whole thing flies apart and comes undone. And there are other aspects where, first of all, if you *try* to pay that much attention and insist on "just this way" about them, you can't even do it. And to the degree you can, you make a mess of things.

Think about any process that you want to undertake, even writing something. There are certain core, central ideas that you really have to get right. You might spend a long time really coming to grips with those things and understanding them. And then there are other things—it's not that you don't care what you say—but you can't, and shouldn't, pay the same amount of finely calibrated attention to those things.

It's the same thing in a meeting, for example. You go to a meeting, and despite what some of the anarchists think, you have to have an agenda [*laughter*], and you have to have some organization to the meeting, or it won't go anywhere. And if people get totally off the subject, you have to insist, "Hey, we are not talking about that, we are talking about this. We can talk about that next, but if we talk about everything at the same time, we're not going to be able to resolve anything." But, on the other hand, while people are talking—and they want to talk from different angles on the subject—you are not going to step in at every point and say, "No, that's not the way to do it, you have to talk about it *this* way." Because, first of all, that's going to be the end of the discussion pretty quickly, and you are not going to have a meeting. Everybody's going to get up and leave. Or never come back after that one meeting. And second of all, you won't have any richness if you try to sit on top of everything everybody says. You will certainly not learn anything that you don't already know. And you will actually undermine some things that you do know.

And you can break all these things down into different levels. Even with the things where you say "this is the point on the agenda," you have to allow a certain flexibility about that, or else people can't express themselves. So, even while on one level you are insisting this is the point on the agenda, on another level you are letting a lot of points come out within that, and allowing a lot of diversity. And sometimes, yes, that crosses over to where people are actually talking about a different point; but if you are too quick to stomp on that, you won't really get good discussion about the point that *is* on the agenda.

So, on one level, you are insisting this is the way it's got to be—for example, this point, and not another point, is what is on the agenda now—but, on another level, you are letting a lot of different things come out in relation to that. And if you don't, you are not only stifling particular people, but you are stifling the process through which a lot of richness is going to come out that you can then synthesize and get the most truth out of.

And you can go on and on with things in life. If you think about anything, you'll realize that there are those things where you really should insist that "this is the way it has to be done, and we have to very finely calibrate this," and many, many things in the same process where you not only *don't have* to do that, but where you *should not* do that.

And this applies especially to the whole realm of working with ideas. If you are going to have a lot of wrangling in society, then you have to have wrangling within the vanguard. While there is a difference between the vanguard and the masses and that shouldn't be obliterated—the people who are part of the conscious vanguard take things up in a different way, and have different structures for how they wrangle with questions—if you make an absolute out of that, and erect just a complete wall between the party and the masses in that regard, you won't get the kind of liveliness that you are seeking.

So you have to determine, even within a party, what are the things over which we absolutely have to have firm unity. Where do we need this "solid core," in other words, and what are the things over which we can have a lot of differences and diversity, and we don't have to put our foot down and resolve it and say it is this way or that way. Every movie you go to, you don't have to have a unified line about that movie. [*laughter*] Things will be awfully boring if you insist on that—and, of course, much more severe problems will arise.

When you are going into a realm of science, there are a lot of questions that are unresolved at any given time among the people who are deeply immersed in that field. Why should you have to step in and—to borrow a metaphor from Mao—the moment you alight from the horse, you start issuing proclamations about what's true and untrue. That's very harmful.

Within a party, you need to have the kind of living process I have been talking about—even while you also definitely need your "solid core." You need "elasticity" on the basis of a solid core. The solid core is principal and essential, but if you don't have the elasticity and a lot of wrangling and diversity on the basis of that, you are going to dry up and you are going to lose everything.

So we can't let go of this solid core. There are things we really do have to insist upon. Think about it. I was having another discussion with another poet, and he was arguing that you really shouldn't suppress ideas, you really have to let all these ideas come out, and then criticize the things that you think are wrong and let people learn. And I said: "Well, that's good as a principle, and it should be applied to a significant degree, but you can't make an absolute out of that." And I gave this example: imagine if you were trying to build a new society, and you go down the street and at every street corner are paintings of women being raped and Black people being lynched. Do you think you could build a new society with those images assaulting people at every turn? Some things you have to put your foot down and say "This will not be allowed, because if it is, the masses of people are going to be demoralized and disoriented, and the reactionaries are going to be emboldened." So there are some things—as I said it's not so simple—there are some things you just cannot allow.

But there are many, many things you can, and should, allow. For example, how do we uproot male supremacy and white supremacy? You can allow a lot of debate about that, and *should* allow a lot of debate about it—and a lot of criticism and struggle over many different things. So there again, you have your solid core, and a lot of elasticity. You have those things where you have to put your foot down and say yes, or no— this is the way it is, and this is the way it is not.

But, again, this "you" needs to be constantly expanding. Still, at any given time, that leading core does have to lead in that way. It does have to correctly combine a solid core with as much elasticity as possible on the basis of that solid core. Even while it is an expanding core, at any given time it has to determine when to hold the reins tightly and pay very detailed attention to things, and what are those conditions and times and circumstances where it is not necessary to do this, and in fact it is better *not* to do so.

Now in this regard it is interesting to think about us in relation to the ruling class. To a significant degree, what is happening in the ruling class in the U.S. at this time is that you have a group of people, open and unabashed reactionaries, that has a very solid core. They are constantly launching attacks on relativism. It's interesting though—a lot of them, the people grouped around Bush, and a lot of the people who want to promote religious fundamentalism—they actually in some ways like to promote post-modernism. Because they *like* relativism in a certain way and up to a certain point. They like it when it is directed against science. [*laughter*] They like it when it argues that science is "just another narrative" that is neither inherently true or not true, but just expresses its own "paradigm." Because then they can promote all kinds of shit like creationism on the basis of having knocked down the idea that science can lead to any truth.

But in general these people hate relativism. And they want to promote absolutes. So they have a certain absolutist solid core, these people that are more—just a short-hand description—grouped around Bush, and in particular those who are part of what we call the Christian Fascist grouping, which has a powerful representation and support from powerful sections of the ruling class.

So they don't really go in for much elasticity. And it's interesting that the sections of the bourgeoisie that do tend to go in for more elasticity, the "liberal" sections of the bourgeoisie—and their reflections among more popular sections of the society—are actually very incapable of answering this absolutism. Their relativism doesn't stand up very well to this absolutism, because it's a relativism without a center, without a solid core. That is, without a center or a solid core that can answer the core assumptions of this other force, this more fascistic force. So the "liberals" are constantly ceding ground to this more fascistic force, because liberalism actually shares many of the same assumptions, and it can't find a solid grounding for its differences. It wants to be the nice guys in the face of very mean-spirited people, and sometimes the latter allow that, with the orientation of "all the better to eat you with." In other words, these more fascistic types are perfectly willing to allow the liberals to be tolerant of them. The problem is, you can't fight a force like this with that kind of tolerance. It's interesting when you hear about things like this new liberal radio station ("Air America") and so on—it's kind of a dud. Because they don't really have an answer.

We do have an answer. But our answer cannot be an absolutist solid core that's just the opposite of theirs in outward form (the "mirror opposite" of it). It has to be one that really is a solid core with a lot of elasticity, and in that way really brings to the fore the actual interests and increasingly the conscious initiative of growing numbers from among the masses of people.

MATERIALISM AND ROMANTICISM: CAN WE DO WITHOUT MYTH? [1]

To get into this subject, I want to quote the following, from Scottish romantic poet Thomas Campbell's "To a Rainbow":

> *"When science from Creation's face*
> *Enchantment's veil withdraws*
> *What lovely visions yield their place*
> *To cold material laws."*

Well, what about this?

First, let's pose and speak to the question: Can we do without myth? Yes—and no. We can and must do without myth which presents itself as reality, which is another way of saying religion. This relates to what is said at the end of *Preaching From a Pulpit of Bones* [2] on what there is in common and what is different between science and religion and art, and in particular the difference between art and religion. Art presents things which are not true, and it tries to draw the audience in to respond to them as if they are true, but at the same time on a more fundamental and larger level, both the people who are making the art and the audience know that what's being presented is not true. (Unless it's documentary films, or "based on a true story," or something like that.)

Most art, particularly art which presents itself as fictional, even if

---

1. This selection is excerpted from the talk *Getting Over the Two Great Humps: Further Thoughts on Conquering the World* and appeared in *Revolutionary Worker* #1211 (August 24, 2003).

2. Avakian, *Preaching from a Pulpit of Bones: We Need Morality, But Not Traditional Morality* (Chicago: Banner Press, 1999), pp. 87-90.

it draws from real events, on the one hand tries to draw the audience into a certain level of accepting it or responding to it as if it is true, while at the same time, on a deeper level and stepping back from it, knowing it's not true. So art presents many fantastic things, and should present many fantastic things, or else it really wouldn't be art. Art couldn't be art if it didn't do that. But, in an ultimate sense, it doesn't pretend that these fantastic things are true. It doesn't try to get its audience to believe, in most cases at least, that these fantastic things are actually real things or events.

On the other hand, as *Preaching* points out, religion presents all kinds of fantastic things but insists that these things are not only true but the essence of truth, and the operative and defining and determining principles of reality. So, in response to the question, "can we do without myth?" the answer is that we have to do without myth in the religious sense, or myth that presents itself as true, myth that presents itself as embodying the defining and organizing principles of reality.

But we can't do without—humanity never could do without and we don't *want* to do without—myth in another sense. To put it another way, we can't and don't want to do without *metaphor*—in art, and in life more broadly. Which is another way of saying that we can't, and don't want to, do without the imagination. Certainly in art, there is a need for metaphor: there is a need for presenting things which are not the same as reality—in particular, reality in any "instant moment" or any immediate aspect of reality—but are larger than life, and more concentrated, as Mao said. There is a need for fiction, there is a need for metaphor—in art and, more broadly speaking, in life.

In this connection, I remember a number of years ago I had a discussion with someone who was really into science fiction. We were talking about this, and I said, I think when we get to future society there won't be a role for science fiction. He said why not? and I answered, because what you would be doing is making predictions about the future based on what you know now and your predictions would almost certainly be wrong. Since then, I have thought about this a number of times and have come to the realization that what I was doing was obliterating the role of art and the role of the imagination. Fortunately, I recognized that before too long. I think this is a useful example, though, of the difference between science and art.

If, in the realm of politics and science, you were to say, "This is what will happen in the future," you would be acting in an irresponsible way if you were not just making certain broad-based predictions, drawing from trends that were already apparent but instead were attempting to paint a whole scenario of what will happen in the future and moreover you were insisting that this be accepted, in all its essential details, as how things *will* actually develop. In other words, if you had no scientific basis to do so, but you presented your predictions not as *science fiction* but as scientific *fact* (or scientifically grounded and completely accurate predictions), then you would be misleading people and you would be irresponsible. But if you write science fiction and present it *as* science fiction and pose possibilities about the future and create scenarios in that sense, there is definitely a role for that in any society and certainly there will be in communist society. This is one form, among many, of giving expression and giving flight to the imagination, which will not only be necessary but very important in terms of the overall character of the society we want and are striving to bring into being.

So there will definitely be a role for metaphor, for the imagination, for myth in that sense—for myth that doesn't present itself as reality. That kind of myth, understood in that sense, we cannot do without, and do not want to do without, and should not try to do without. Myth that presents itself as reality, however—myth that takes on, in one form or another, the character of religion—we can and must do without. But, to return to the lines from the poem I cited above, *when science withdraws the veil from creation's face*—when we can give scientific explanations for natural phenomena and we adopt a scientific method for approaching natural phenomena—are we then left only with "cold material laws"? No.

No in two senses. First of all, material laws are not so "cold," as we have discovered. If you are a dialectical materialist, you know that laws represent tendencies, tendential phenomena, not something iron and monolithic and without contradiction. They represent tendencies that are contradicted by other tendencies, or come into contradiction with other tendencies, and they themselves are the expression of contradiction, motion and struggle. Laws are not "cold"; even real material laws are not "cold" material laws.

Real science is not "cold." It is different than art, and the role of imagination in science (as I will speak to in a second) is different than it is in art. But as many scientists, particularly the better ones, have pointed out (I believe Einstein made this point too), there is no good science without the imagination. There is definitely a role for the imagination in science, even though science is, in its essence, an explanation of reality and of the motive forces in reality. But that should not be, in its best and highest expression, "cold," stiff, rigid and undialectical.

"Material laws" or materialism should be dialectical and full of life and vitality. So, even on that level, there is nothing that should be "cold" about materialism. Understanding the real world and the driving forces in it is an ongoing process and ongoing struggle, overcoming the contradiction between ignorance and knowledge, between the new and the old, and so on. It is a lively, vigorous process in which there is a great role for the imagination. There is nothing "cold" or dead or rigid or "grey" about it whatsoever, if it is understood in the most scientific sense.

This harks back to the error in our polemic against the Mensheviks concerning the Chinese mathematician who was studying the Goldbach conjecture. In a previous talk I made the point that the way we dealt with this in our answer to the Mensheviks[3] involved a tendency toward philistinism and what could be characterized as vulgar materialism.

Now, this was a minor aspect of our struggle against the Mensheviks. I don't want to blow it out of proportion, and I'm certainly not trying to reverse verdicts on our struggle against the Mensheviks and the revisionist coup in China. But there is a lesson I'm trying to draw from this relatively minor error. The lesson is that there is an importance to "pure research," to "pure science"; and there is a way in which that is analogous to the need for myth, as I have spoken to it—to the need for the imagination, the need for metaphor, the need for poetry.

Again, even in the scientific realm itself, while its essence is bring-

---

3. This refers to an argument in a polemic against those formerly in the RCP (dubbed "Mensheviks" because of their opportunist position and methods) who supported the reactionary coup and restoration of capitalism in China, led by Deng Xiaoping after the death of Mao. This argument vulgarized what is involved in the Goldbach conjecture and essentially said that trying to solve this mathematical problem is a complete waste of time and resources. See "How the Mensheviks Take Revisionism as the Key Link," in *Revolution and Counter-revolution: The Revisionist Coup in China and the Struggle in the Revolutionary Communist Party, USA* (Chicago: RCP Publications, 1978), p. 280, and "The Correct Approach to Intellectuals...Engels Got Upset When Duhring Was Removed From His University Post," *Revolutionary Worker* #1226 (January 25, 2004), from *Getting Over the Two Great Humps: Further Thoughts on Conquering the World*, a talk given in the late 1990s that was excerpted in the *Revolutionary Worker* from October 1997 through January 1998 and from October 2003 through January 2004. It is available online at revcom.us.

ing to light reality and the motive forces in reality, there is a need for philosophy in science, along with imagination. There is a need for people to pursue the philosophical questions about the nature of reality and the motive forces of reality. There is a need for them to research things, including particular aspects of reality, particular aspects of the motive forces in reality, that don't have immediate bearing on practical needs and concerns of the time, whether economic or social or political.

Of course, among the intellectuals there will be a tendency, and at times a very strong tendency, to want to run wild with that, and to divorce theory in an overall way from practice. But the fact that in our epistemological understanding, in our theory of knowledge, we recognize that practice is decisive, not only in changing the world but also in knowing it, shouldn't cause us to reduce materialism to "cold" mechanical materialism, where there must always be a one-to-one relation, where theory must always be, in the most narrow and immediate sense, directly linked to and in the service of practice. In the overall dialectical relation between practice and theory, in that overall dynamic, practice is the decisive link, even for knowing as well as for changing the world. But again, that doesn't obliterate the need for aspects of theory that are not related, in the most narrow and immediate sense, to practical concerns or to practice itself in a general sense. There is a need for exploration, investigation, research in its own right, as well as there is a need in an overall and fundamental sense for theory to be linked with, to be grounded in, to be returned to, and to be in the service of practice—of not simply knowing but transforming the world.

The Importance of Poetry and a Poetic Spirit

All this is related to some statements by Mao that were cited and commented on in "End/Beginning."[4] There it quotes Mao saying: "Whenever the mind becomes rigid, it is very dangerous." That's a very pithy statement, and I think it's worth pondering long and deeply: "Whenever the mind becomes rigid, it is very dangerous." Then Mao goes on to say: "Unless you have a conquering spirit it is very dangerous to study Marxism-Leninism." This is another of those pithy and provocative statements by Mao.

And "End/Beginning" quotes Mao further: "If you are too realistic

---

4. Avakian, "The End of a Stage—the Beginning of a New Stage," dated late 1989, *Revolution*, No. 60 (Fall 1990), p. 16.

you can't write poetry." Here Mao is expressing the dialectical relation between realism and romanticism. He says if you are *too* realistic you can't write poetry. He's not calling for idealism in place of materialism. But his statement is emphasizing from another angle the importance of the imagination and giving flight to the imagination, as well as the importance of poetry, and all that poetry symbolizes or represents. In other words, why is he saying this—if poetry is unimportant who cares if you can't write it? Obviously, he is saying that poetry is an important part of life. It's an important part of the kind of movement we are building. It's an important part of the kind of society we are struggling to bring into being.

And then, after citing these statements from Mao in "End/Beginning," it goes on to add: "in keeping with the thrust of what Mao is saying here, if you don't have a poetic spirit—or at least a poetic side—it is very dangerous for you to lead a Marxist movement or be the leader of a socialist state." This goes along with Mao's points that if a mind is rigid it is very dangerous, unless you have a conquering spirit it is very dangerous to study MLM, and if you are too realistic you can't write poetry. A Marxist movement, a revolutionary struggle and its MLM vanguard, a socialist state and its leadership, must have a poetic side and a poetic spirit at the same time as they are thoroughly grounded in a scientific appreciation of reality and its motion and development.

So, do we want everything reduced to "cold material laws"? No. Even with regard to "material laws," we have to recognize this is a vibrant, vital, living matter of dialectical materialism.

This relates to the way *Preaching From a Pulpit of Bones* ends with a reference to a statement by "The Amazing Randi," who has made it his life's work to take on and debunk all these various charlatans—people who are promoting ESP and spoon-benders and other kinds of people like that. He makes the point—he isn't speaking directly to religion *per se*, but it's clear that this includes religion, or certainly we can legitimately interpret what he says to apply to all religion (as well as to things like parapsychology, ESP, astrology, and other stuff like that)—that just because you give up belief in all these kinds of superstition, doesn't mean that life becomes dull, lifeless, and boring. There is plenty of excitement to be had in trying to "take in" and comprehend and reflect about the *real* world and all the things that happen in reality as it actually is. There is a tremendous role for the imagination, there is a tremendous excitement to be had from contemplating and wrestling with reality in (as we would say) all its complexity and contradictory motion and development. You don't have to resort to inventing things and pretending that they're real in order for there to be a tremendous role for awe and wonder.

This is an important point Randi was making, and that's why *Preaching* ends with that point. This speaks to the argument that this Scottish romantic poet Campbell was making: if we give up belief in supernatural things, things beyond the realm of reality, everything is going to become cold and lifeless—we're going to be giving up something vital about the human condition, about the essence of human beings, that we want to hang onto. But that is not true.

It's going to be a challenge, going back to what Mao said about the importance of having a poetic spirit—the fact that if you are too realistic you can't write poetry and the implied fact that poetry is important in life, in the society that we are striving for and in the movement that is struggling to bring that society into being—there is going to be a challenge of how to handle this poetic aspect in dialectical relation, first of all, to the material base of society:

- How to handle the need to allow for and to encourage a certain amount of pure research in the scientific realm in relation to the material-economic base of society and the need for development and transformation of that economic-material base, and for meeting the needs of the people, including their material needs at any given time.
- How to handle scientific inquiry, and the allotment of material resources and people to that inquiry, in dialectical relation not only to the material base of society and the material needs of the masses of people *but also* to the realities of the class struggle, both within the country and internationally.

These are difficult and complex contradictions. It's going to be a real challenge to correctly handle this dialectical relation and to meet the material and political requirements of the proletarian state and the proletarian revolution while giving expression and encouragement to the poetic aspect, understood broadly to encompass the imagination and metaphor and all the things that can be emblematic of this whole aspect of things. This is something that we will have to continually come back to, and learn more deeply how to handle. It's going to be profoundly and at times intensely posed all along the way in the struggle to advance to the epoch of communism.

Now, obviously, what I've been talking about here involves the question of religion and "spirituality" (or "soul," as it is sometimes referred to) and its relation to dialectical materialism, which represents a comprehensively and systematically scientific approach to reality and the motive forces in reality. Here we can refer to the statement that is frequently cited, taken from the Christian Bible, that man (or people) "cannot live by bread alone." Communism recognizes and embraces this. This harks back to what was said in response to the Scottish romantic poet Campbell. Communism and its dialectical materialist outlook and method do not leave us with nothing but "cold material laws."

It is ironic—and an outrageous irony—that the bourgeoisie and its apologists, who are really the coldest "materialists" of all, often and generally accuse communists of being the ones who don't recognize, or refuse to allow for, the fact that people cannot live by bread alone. This was expressed, for example, by Zbigniew Brzezinski in his critique of communism—his "explanation" for the "demise of communism" with the break-up of the Soviet Union and its bloc—which was answered in *Phony Communism is Dead...*[5] (Despite the fact that I believe there is a certain shortcoming in that answer to Brzezinski in *Phony*, I'm certainly not saying that Brzezinski was right after all, or that our answer wasn't very much to the point and very thorough in refuting him. There is just a minor aspect of that answer that perhaps should have been approached somewhat differently, in line with the need to be thoroughly dialectical as well as thoroughly materialist.) People like Brzezinski and similar types, as well as religious leaders—and not only the most reactionary ones but even generally progressive religious people like Jim Wallis who wrote the book *The Soul of Politics* which is spoken to in *Preaching*—make this fundamental criticism of communism: it doesn't recognize that "people cannot live by bread alone." It doesn't recognize that there is an essential and necessary quality of human existence and of human nature, as they would describe it, which involves a striving for spirituality, a striving for something greater than "cold material reality." Communism, they say, cannot recognize, embrace, and fulfill this.

Of course, everyone from the pope to "popular commentators" generally misuses the concept of materialism to identify it essentially with two things: one, some sort of crass consumerism and "consump-

---

5. Avakian, *Phony Communism Is Dead...Long Live Real Communism!*, 2nd edition (Chicago: RCP Publications, 2004), pp. 55-74.

tionism," and, two, a mechanical materialist approach to reality, the kind that is criticized in the lines cited from the poem by the Scottish romantic poet Campbell. This was, to a significant degree, one of the driving forces of the romantic poets generally: their reaction against the industrial revolution and even a rejection of some of the scientific aspects of the Enlightenment. These Romantics were a very complicated and mixed bag, because they joined in important struggles against oppression at the time, but they had this critique of the industrial revolution, and even of a scientific approach to reality, such as it was at that time (limited as it was by the bourgeois world outlook). This is a complex phenomenon, and I don't want to back into a whole discussion of that. But a common characteristic of the critique of "materialism" that is brought forward by everyone from the pope to poets and others with a "romantic" and "mystical" approach, is to reduce materialism to the phenomenon of crass consumerism (or consumptionism) and the method of mechanical materialism. And often in such critiques these things are mixed together, so that materialism in general is identified with both consumerism and "cold" mechanical materialism. And this latter aspect in particular is frequently emphasized in the critique of Marxist materialism.

The "Spiritual" in a Cold and Heartless World

Here, again, is the question of "spirit" and "spirituality" and how this relates to a scientific view of reality. When today people use the word "spiritual," they are not necessarily intending this in a religious sense—or at least a more conventional religious sense—although some are. More generally, this refers to a longing for something with "heart" in a world that seems increasingly heartless. For a positive connection with other people, in opposition to the increasing atomization and competitiveness that is promoted by the workings of the prevailing order. For a link, a bond, with something beyond one's self, beyond the selfish and narrow interests and the dog-eat-dog mentality and relations which are assuming such pronounced form in contemporary capitalist society. For a belief in something greater than the petty and paltry concerns and mean-spirited motivations that are promoted in this society.

In *The Demon-Haunted World: Science as a Candle in the Dark*, Carl Sagan speaks to this question of spirit and its relation to matter:

" 'Spirit' comes from the Latin word 'to breathe.' What we breathe is air, which is certainly matter, however thin.

Despite usage to the contrary, there is no necessary implica-
tion in the word 'spiritual' that we are talking of anything
other than matter (including the matter of which the brain
is made), or anything outside the realm of science. On occa-
sion, I will feel free to use the word. Science is not only
compatible with spirituality; it is a profound source of spirituality. When we recognize our place in an immensity of
light-years and in the passage of ages, when we grasp the
intricacy, beauty, and subtlety of life, then that soaring feeling, that sense of elation and humility combined, is surely
spiritual. So are our emotions in the presence of great art or
music or literature, or of acts of exemplary selfless courage
such as those of Mohandas Gandhi or Martin Luther King,
Jr. The notion that science and spirituality are somehow
mutually exclusive does a disservice to both."[6]

Here we can recognize that even such concepts as "beauty" and
acts of "exemplary selfless courage" have *a social content* and are seen
differently by people with different class outlooks: class-conscious proletarians would choose examples other than Gandhi and King, who
never represented and in fact opposed the need for thoroughgoing radical transformation and the revolutionary movement and ideology necessary to bring that about. But, despite the fact that Sagan's outlook is
not that of the proletariat, his comments on spirituality and
matter/materialism contain much that we can agree with, much that is
insightful and important.

At the same time, in applying the most thoroughly and comprehensively scientific outlook and method—dialectical and historical
materialism—representing the viewpoint of the proletariat, when we
talk about the quest for "spirituality," the first thing we have to say is
that this can't be understood or approached in abstraction from, or by
ignoring, the social relations in which this is actually situated. There is
this yearning of many people which seems to be acutely and broadly felt
these days—a yearning for some sort of firm moral principles to deal
with a lot of the madness that is out there. There is also a certain feeling of emptiness and of a spiritual void (this is often how people
express it) and a need to fill this void. But we can't divorce this from,

---

6. Carl Sagan, *The Demon-Haunted World: Science as a Candle in the Dark* (New
York: Random House, 1996) pp. 29-30.

first of all, the prevailing social relations and their foundation in the economic-production relations in society (and the world as a whole), which shape people's individual life conditions as well as their larger social interactions. And, more particularly, we can't divorce this from the parasitism of imperialism as well as the upheavals that it is creating—upheavals and struggles that the domination of imperialism and the operation of the imperialist process of accumulation are creating in Third World countries as well as in imperialist countries. Particularly in talking about the middle strata, and more especially the privileged strata in the imperialist countries, this feeling of alienation that many people experience can in no way be divorced from all this and in particular from the whole deepening phenomenon of parasitism.

I remember years ago riding on an airplane next to some guy who was a lower level executive in some corporation. He got in my ear and started telling me all about his life experiences—he was going to give me "the word," because he had turned to religion, to fundamentalist Christianity. I let him go on for awhile, and I learned some things from what he was talking about, but then I made it clear I wasn't really interested in being proselytized for his religion. But it was interesting to learn why he had been pulled toward this. He had been relatively successful, financially and in terms of status, in his work; he had the home in the suburbs, the cars, and all that. He was working long hours, staying late on the job—and, he admitted, he was cheating on his wife. But "at the end of the day" it was all empty. He felt an emptiness, and he was increasingly turning to drinking and this and that. Religion—fundamentalist Christian religion in this case—gave him a certain renewed moral sense—it brought him back to a more "traditional morality," because a contradiction had developed in his life between the traditional morality in which he had been indoctrinated and to which he still adhered on one level, and his actual practice, his personal behavior, which was in conflict with that on many different levels. This religion brought him back to "traditional morality" and was, in a short-term and narrow sense, a way of resolving that contradiction. It filled a certain void that he was feeling—this life he was leading, with all its so-called "success," as measured by the prevailing standards of society, left a void, an emptiness.

What was striking to me then and is striking about this phenomenon more broadly, especially now, in the U.S. as well as in other countries, is how this is very much related to the parasitism of imperialism, which of course is deepening in this period and is very much bound up with the "high-tech revolution." As it was put in *Strategic Questions*[7] (and this formulation was also used by Clark Kissinger independently of *SQ*) the position of significant strata in the imperialist countries today is fairly "high up" on the "world food chain"—this is another way of giving expression to their parasitic position.

The alienation that broad numbers of people in contemporary society feel is not reducible to being an expression of parasitism, for all strata and for all people, because a feeling of alienation also exists among people who are among the proletariat and the exploited of the world. But certainly among the middle class, and especially the more privileged strata, there is a very strong relationship between this feeling of alienation and spiritual malaise and the parasitism of their social position, especially in the imperialist countries. And it is important to recognize how religion rationalizes and provides a "salve" for this. It eases the pain and the feeling of alienation without calling upon and requiring people to give up parasitism and privilege and to struggle against the system that is so deeply rooted in this parasitism (as Lenin said, imperialism puts the seal of parasitism broadly and deeply on the whole of imperialist society). Religion, especially in the form which most appeals to the privileged strata, provides a certain salve for that without really requiring people to make any transformation, even in their individual lives, in terms of giving up this parasitic position, let alone struggling to overturn the exploitative and oppressive relations in society as a whole, of which this parasitism is an integral part.

That's one of the key roles that religion plays for people in that particular position. It rationalizes their parasitism. It gives them a rationalization and speaks to their malaise, without actually requiring them to strike at the cause of the malaise.

At the same time, there is among the basic masses tremendous and increasing suffering and upheaval and a feeling of being uprooted, both materially and ideologically-morally, in societies such as the U.S. and in the world as a whole. For the great majority of people in the world, there is tremendous suffering. The massive upheaval and dislocations of the peasantry and the migration to the cities in the Third World—or within the imperialist countries, all the chaos and madness,

---

7. See "A Problem of Strategic Orientation for the Revolution: The Two 90/10's," *RW* #890 (January 19, 1997). *Strategic Questions* is another talk given by Bob Avakian. Excerpts appeared in *Revolutionary Worker* #881 and #884-893 (November 1996 through February 1997), and in *RW* #1176-78 (November 24 through December 8, 2002). They are available online at revcom.us.

the uncertainty and the volatility of life conditions and modes of existence for significant sections of the people, and in a particularly pronounced way among the youth—all this too can give rise to the feeling of a need for some kind of spirituality. A need for something that can create some meaning out of all this madness, that can give some sense of purpose in the midst of all this chaos. That can also give some feeling of relief amidst all the desperation and misery.

Religion as a Narcotic—An "Opiate of the People"

This speaks very directly to the role of religion as an "opiate," as Marx originally said. In this regard, as I was reading Lenin's writings during the first few, desperate years of the Soviet republic, focusing on his comments about the open, unblemished, and unrestricted exercise of dictatorship, I came across something that struck me as very interesting in regard to this question of religion and "spirituality." Lenin speaks to how Feuerbach had given a very good answer to those who said that the masses need religion to ease their suffering. As Lenin characterized it, Feuerbach made the point that slaves don't need consolation for their suffering—they need to rise up against their enslavement and torment—*and* giving them "consolation" in the way religion does *works against* their rising up to cast off their enslavement. And, after all, if you think about it, that's what an "opiate" is. Even if some who "push" this "opiate" are well-intentioned and see their role more as providing "morphine" to help people get through the pain (or hallucinogenic "inspiration" to see beyond the pain) ultimately it still comes down to the fact that, in giving this kind of "relief" and "diversion," you are actually working *against* the slave rising up to cast off the conditions which give rise to the *feeling* of the *need* for some kind of consolation.

This was really Marx's point. Marx spoke to this in a very dialectical and all-sided way. He goes on, after saying that religion is an "opiate," to say that it is the "heart of a heartless world." So there you see he is speaking to the fact that this kind of cold bourgeois society is a society without real heart—or without "soul," using that in a broad, and not a narrow, religious, sense. People are searching for something beyond the cold material exploitation and oppression that characterizes bourgeois society and the mentality that goes along with and is promoted by that—the reducing of everything to the cash nexus, the treating of everything, including people, as something to be merely possessed and used to advance yourself at the expense of others. This gives rise to its opposite, both in the material sphere but also ideologically. It gives rise to a striving for something beyond that kind of actual cold material exploitation and oppression and "commodification" of everything. Religion, however, provides not a real cure for this, but an opiate for it. That's the point. It doesn't provide a cure because it doesn't lead people to actually rise up and overthrow the conditions that give rise to the feeling of a need for consolation and for some sort of heart in a heartless world. Religion instead reinforces the *acceptance* of these conditions. That's what Marx was saying by speaking to its narcotic role.

Check out people who become "born-again," in the religious sense. They come off very much like people who have become addicted to narcotics. It has the same kind of effect on people, including people from different strata who have come to religion from differing places, for differing reasons.

A Back-Handed Tribute to Communism

This relates to the whole "resurgence" of religion in the U.S. But also very much related to this "resurgence of religion," in countries such as the U.S., as well as more generally, is in fact the so-called "demise of communism." And in this light, once again, we can see how much capitalism *needs* religion. We see that, for example, once the mask of socialism was thrown off in the Soviet Union and its empire, religion came flourishing out and is now openly promoted by the bourgeoisie there, including former "communists." The resurgence of religion, especially with the declared "demise of communism," is not only an expression of how much capitalism needs religion but, in a significant aspect (as also pointed out in *Preaching*), it is also a kind of "back-handed tribute" to communism. It represents a recognition that the world of capitalism is in fact a *miserable* world and that communism holds out the only hope for a much better world, in this real world, not only materially but ideologically (or spiritually, using that word in the sense that has been discussed here). It is a recognition of this objectively—and, on the part of many people who have retreated into religion from a more progressive, or more radical, or even a more revolutionary and optimistic viewpoint, it is also, in an important aspect, subjectively a recognition—that only communism represents the road to a radically different and better world than the "cold" and heartless world of capitalism. If and to the degree that people have, in the short run at least, been convinced to give up on communism as such a radical alter-native, then the attractiveness of religion grows, as an illusory means of seeking an alternative to, and/or relief from, the heartlessness and cold-ness of this capitalist-dominated world.

We should recognize the important aspect in which this is actual-ly a back-handed tribute to communism—a reflection of the fact that revolution and communism represents the only way there can actually be a better world, both in terms of the relations among people and in terms of the guiding principles and morality of people. We should turn that into a very positive thing; we should grasp and act on the under-standing that it underlines the need to very boldly put forward and popularize what communism actually represents and how it holds out the prospect of overcoming, *in the real world*, all material relations of exploitation, oppression, inequality, parasitism, and all the violence and brutality that inevitably is bound up with these material relations, as well as their reflection in the mind (and "spirit").

Awe and Wonder...The Need To Be Amazed

Communism is not about doing away with "spirit"—in the mate-rialist sense. It is not about doing away with the imagination, and with awe and wonder. These are essential qualities of human existence. Without descending and degenerating into bourgeois theories of "human nature," we can say that there are certain qualities that define human beings in a broad sense. Understood with dialectical material-ism, there are certain qualities about human beings that flow from their character, from the character of the species and its intellectual abilities as well as its material conditions. One of these qualities is what could be characterized as "the need to be amazed." In something I read that one of our comrades had written, it talked about "the need to be amazed"—that this is an important part, an essential part, of the quali-ties of human beings that we have to recognize. Communism can more fully give expression to this than any other ideology and social system. This is really what's being spoken to at the end of *Preaching From a Pul-pit of Bones,* in particular with the reference to (with the citing of) the statement by "The Amazing Randi": there is plenty to amaze us in reality.

In art we do need things presented which are other than reality. In general, in art, in science, and in life overall, we need to unleash and give much fuller flight to the imagination. We need to recognize and give expression to the need of people to be amazed.

People look at what religion calls "the heavens." They look at the stars, the galaxies. They can see a small part of the vastness of the universe, and they can imagine the greater vastness of the universe. Or they can look on a small scale, look with a microscope and see a small microbe or whatever, and be amazed by what goes on internally within that. They can ponder the relation between what you can see with a microscope and what you can see with a telescope. This is an essential quality of human beings. Human beings will always strive for this. Far from trying to suppress this, or failing to recognize it, we can and should and will give much fuller expression to it.

Communism will not put an end to—nor somehow involve the suppression of—awe and wonder, the imagination, and "the need to be amazed." On the contrary, it will give much greater, and increasing, scope to this. It will give flight on a much grander scale to the imagination, in dialectical relation with—and in an overall sense as a part of—a systematic and comprehensive scientific outlook and method for comprehending and transforming reality.

We have to understand that there is a unity there. Yes, it is a unity of opposites, but overall there is a unity between a systematic and comprehensive scientific outlook and method for comprehending and transforming reality, and giving flight to the imagination and giving expression to the "need to be amazed." Communism can achieve and continually re-achieve a much higher synthesis on this than anything previously in human experience.

There is an opposition—but, again, it is a dialectical opposition, involving identity as well as difference—between science and the imagination, so that each can and should inspire and strengthen the other; and there is, in fact, each within the other. There is imagination within science, and there is science within the imagination. Even the most unscientific imagination can't avoid having some science within it, and even the "driest" science cannot be literally devoid of all imagination. This certainly should be, and will be, all the more the case with the most thoroughly scientific outlook, communism, the more fully its critical and revolutionary essence is unleashed and applied, even now and in a qualitatively greater way in communist society itself.

BOB AVAKIAN IN A DISCUSSION WITH COMRADES ON EPISTEMOLOGY: ON KNOWING AND CHANGING THE WORLD [1]

"Everything that is actually true is good for the proletariat, all truths can help us get to communism."

—*Bob Avakian*

Editors' Note: The following is based on a discussion by Bob Avakian with some comrades on the subject of epistemology. Epistemology refers to a theory of knowledge, to an understanding of how people acquire knowledge, what is the nature of truth and how people come to know the truth. In what follows an effort has been made to retain the original character of what was said and how it was recorded: these were not prepared remarks by Chairman Avakian (or the other comrades) but are comments that were made in the course of a discussion, and what follows here is based on notes that were taken of that discussion. These were not verbatim (exact word-for-word) notes, but were typed up at the time and then gone over for sense and minor corrections by a participant of the meeting. Not every contribution by every comrade has been included; but there are parts which respond to or expand upon a point made by Chairman Avakian that are helpful and so they were included for publication. This was further edited for publication.

* * * * *

Bob Avakian: It does focus up a lot of questions, this attitude toward the intellectuals. From the time of *Conquer the World*[2] (*CTW*) I

---

1. This selection was first published in *Revolutionary Worker* #1262 (December 19, 2004).

2. Avakian, *Conquer the World? The International Proletariat Must and Will* (*Revolution*, No. 50, December 1981).

have been bringing forward an epistemological rupture with a lot of the history of the ICM [International Communist Movement], including China and the GPCR [Great Proletarian Cultural Revolution], which had this thing arguing that there is such a thing as proletarian truth and bourgeois truth—this was in a major circular[3] put out by the leadership of the Chinese Communist Party. In some polemics we wrote around the coup in China, we uncritically echoed this. Later on, we criticized ourselves for that. This rupture actually began with *CTW*. *CTW* was an epistemological break—we have to go for the truth, rather than hiding things, etc.—a whole approach of interrogating our whole history. That's why it was taken as a breath of fresh air by some, while other people hated it, saying it reduced the history of the international communist movement and our banner of communism to a "tattered flag"— which was not the point at all. *End to the Horror*[4] has a whole point that there is no such thing as class truth, but there is a methodology that lets you get at the truth more fully; the open letters to Sagan and Gould (and Isaac Asimov) wrestled with this more fully.[5] Then there is the point I have been stressing by referring to, and expressing some agreement with, the argument of John Stuart Mill on contesting of ideas—on the importance of people being able to hear arguments not just as they are characterized by those who oppose them but as they are put forward by those who strongly believe in them. It is not that Mao never had any of this approach, but still what I have been bringing forward represents an epistemological break. Even though many people welcomed *CTW* on one level, it divided into two again, and that division became sharper as things went on. I was pursuing *CTW* where it was taking me, I didn't have an a priori understanding [a priori here refers to forming conclusions in advance of investigating something]. There's a logic to what I was pursuing in *CTW*—it takes you to a certain place, and if you resist that you go to another place. There's been a clinging to this old way the communist movement has approached these questions, epito-

---

3. "Circular of the Central Committee of the Chinese Communist Party," dated May 16, 1966, in *Important Documents on the Great Proletarian Cultural Revolution in China* (Peking: Foreign Languages Press, 1970).

4. Avakian, *A Horrible End, or An End to the Horror?* (Chicago: RCP Publications, 1984).

5. "Some Questions to Carl Sagan and Stephen Gould" and "More Questions to Carl Sagan, Stephen Gould, and Isaac Asimov" in Avakian, *Reflections, Sketches and Provocations: Essays and Commentary, 1981-1987* (Chicago: RCP Publications, 1990).

mized in class truth—this is still a real problem.

Your attitude towards intellectuals has to do with the philosophical question of what you think we're trying to do, and what is it the proletariat represents. What is the "godlike position of the proletariat," as I referred to it in *Strategic Questions*?[6] On one level, you're sort of sitting on a hill watching this procession go by of the development of humanity. Some of it you can see more dimly and some more clearly— you look at this whole sweep and then at a certain point this group called the proletariat emerges from within this set of social relations that can take it to a particular place, to a whole different world. But you shouldn't reify the proletariat: Yes, it's made up of real people, but it's not a matter of individual proletarians but of the proletariat as a class, of its position in society and of where its interests lie, in the most fundamental sense, as a class. On another level, looking at the sweep of history, you see the role of intellectuals as well. Are they basically making trouble for us? This is how some people see it—and this has been a definite tendency, and real problem, in the history of our movement.

But from the standpoint of a sweeping view of history, you look at this a different way. For example, there is this physicist Brian Greene who has written some books popularizing questions of physics, and he speaks to this big contradiction the physicists can't yet resolve between relativity and quantum mechanics, so the question they're facing is: how do you get the next level of synthesis? What do we think of that— is that a big waste of time unless we can use that narrowly? Yes, people like this, people in these fields generally, need to be struggled with— but in a good way. If we were working in the right way in these spheres we'd be having a lot of good struggle with people around all kinds of questions, including questions arising in their work, but first of all we would be seriously engaging the work they are doing and the questions

---

6. The section of *Strategic Questions*, another talk by Bob Avakian, that discusses the "godlike position of the proletariat" has not been published. The concept is discussed in "Fighting Not Just for Revenge But To Emancipate All Humanity" from *Great Objectives and Grand Strategy* in *RW* #1140 (February 24, 2002) and "Holding Firmly to Basic Principles—But Not Being Bound by Convention or Superstition" from *Grasp Revolution, Promote Production: Questions of Outlook and Method, Some Points on the New Situation* in *RW* #1186 (February 9, 2003), available online at revcom.us. It is also discussed in another essay in this volume, "The 'Godlike Position of the Proletariat,' The Sweep of History." Excerpts from *Strategic Questions* appeared in *Revolutionary Worker* #881 and #884-893 (November 1996 through February 1997), and in *RW* #1176-78 (November 24 through December 8, 2002). They are available online at revcom.us.

they are wrestling with. We would do this in a different way than it's often been done in the history of our movement. Is it important for what we're trying to accomplish, or should be trying to accomplish, whether these physicists understand more about the world? Yes. Do they need "loose reins" to accomplish this? Yes. Do we need to struggle with them? Yes. Do we need to have them come down and learn from the masses? Yes. But there is a legitimate part to the point that Bill Martin has made, in an introduction to a book that will be coming out soon—consisting of a conversation between him and me—the point that, yes, there are problems of intellectuals getting isolated in their ivory towers but at the same time there is a definite need for intellectuals to have the right atmosphere and space in which to do their work.[7]

Yes, we have to get down from the mountain and get with the masses, but you have to go up to the mountain too or we won't do anything good. Stalin—some of his errors are his own, resulting to a large degree from his methodological problems, and some of it was carried forward from Lenin (I spoke to some of this in *CTW*).

That stuff [a narrow view] on intellectuals has pretty much been the conventional wisdom in our movement, including in the Great Proletarian Cultural Revolution. But for a couple of decades there's been a clear motion of what I've been fighting for that's going in a different way. Do you recognize that, or do you reject that and go for something else? There are different lines and roads represented by this. XXX [a leading comrade in the RCP] said to me, one of the most important things is for you to do what you do; but I said at least as important is for *you* to do this too. We need a solid core united around the correct line—and if we don't have that, then it's not gonna be good if people take a lot of initiative. If people are with this, we'll unleash a lot of stuff and it'll go in different directions, even funny directions, but we'll struggle and get somewhere.

How do you put your arms around the history of humanity? What about these indigenous people whose religion is so crucial to their sense of identity? Difficult—but we don't have a shot without this kind of outlook and methodology I'm arguing for. Without this, you're either

---

7. Bill Martin is a social theorist and professor of philosophy at DePaul University, Chicago. His numerous books include: *Politics in the Impasse* (1996), *The Radical Project: Sartrean Investigations* (2001), and *Avant Rock* (2002). The book *Marxism and the Call of the Future: Conversations on Ethics, History, and Politics* (Chicago: Open Court, 2005) by Bob Avakian and Bill Martin had not yet been published at the time of this discussion.

gonna uncritically tail this or brutally suppress it when it gets in the way. Mao had some sense of this. He sharply criticized the Soviet Union's policy of forcing people to raise pigs in the Moslem areas. But we need to go further with this. Mao's been dead for thirty years and Lenin eighty—what are we doing if we don't go beyond them?

This was a beginning rupture, an epistemological break, that was represented by *CTW*. The point is to change the world, and we need to understand reality. Darwin and Newton brought forth some understanding of reality. This has been shown to be limited and wrong in some ways, particularly in the case of Newton—Darwin was basically correct, and it's very important to uphold this, especially in the face of attacks on evolution by religious fundamentalists, but the understanding of evolution has progressed beyond Darwin. Yes, we don't want people in ivory towers, but Bill Martin's point on this [that intellectuals do need the setting in which to do their work]—we have to solve that contradiction. We have to put this problem to the masses. And if we don't solve it right, even after power has been seized and we're leading a socialist society, the people will overthrow us or sit aside when a bigger army comes in. Saddam Hussein is an example: he was an oppressor of the people, and while the people didn't overthrow him, they also didn't rise to defend him when a more powerful oppressor, the U.S. imperialists, invaded to get rid of him. That will happen to us if we don't solve the real problems—including the day-to-day problems of the masses—in socialist society, but we have to lead the masses and even struggle with these intermediate strata by putting the contradictions to them. Here's how we're dealing with this, what's your criticism of that? As opposed to bringing out the army to suppress things. I'm no idealist—sometimes you do need the army—but it shouldn't be the first thing you reach for. You have to pose the contradictions and ask: what's your idea for how to solve this? Here people are going without health care, and how do we solve that without reproducing the same gross inequalities so that a few people can do their work in the sciences, and on the other hand so that people in the sciences aren't stopped from their work. Or what is your solution to dealing with imperialist encirclement of our socialist state? Here's the contradiction—let's wrangle with it. How do we handle this?

It's not like Mao didn't have a lot of that, but it's a little bit different way, what I'm putting forward. You trust the masses that if you put the problems to them you can struggle with them, learn from them, lead them and win a big section of the masses as you do this. I don't want to be by myself on this road—that's no good, that won't take things where they need to go—I want more people on this road, enabling me to do work and doing work themselves. Many people here and people in our Party and more people beyond the Party can contribute to all this. This is a very good process. In response to a talk I gave, *Elections, Democracy and Dictatorship, Resistance and Revolution,*[8] a professor, referring to my criticisms of Stalin and his methodology, and the need for us to do better than this, raised that it wouldn't have been such a problem if Stalin had had people around him who would challenge him; and this professor went on to put forward: "Here's my challenge—how would you do better than in the Soviet Union in the 1920s and '30s and China in the GPCR?" And he elaborated on this: "Here's how I see the problem: people are gonna start speaking out against you when you're in power, and pretty soon you're gonna bring out the army and suppress them." This is an important point—a real contradiction—and there needs to be ongoing dialogue about that with people like this, and more generally. I believe we can find a good resolution to this contradiction—but it won't be easy, it will take real work and struggle, all the way through, to handle this correctly.

Here is a big problem: when the time comes, when there is a revolutionary situation, our material force has to be able to meet and defeat the imperialists, it has to be the leading force in doing that, so that we can get the solid core and then open things up. If you open up the basic question of socialism to an electoral contest, you'll sink the ship. We have to bring forward the material force to defeat the enemy and set the terms for the new society. Then we have to do all this other stuff, to "open the society up" and lead the masses in accordance with this—that's the whole point on the moving process of solid core and elasticity. [This refers to the concept and approach of "a solid core with a lot of elasticity," which Chairman Avakian has been giving emphasis to—a principle he insists should be applied in socialist society as well as to the revolutionary process overall, aiming for the final goal of a communist world.] [9]

This question of "solid core with a lot of elasticity" is not some-

---

8. Audio files of this talk are available on the web at bobavakian.net.

9. For more on this, see the talk by Bob Avakian, *Dictatorship and Democracy, and the Socialist Transition to Communism.* The full text of this talk is available online at revcom.us, and selections from this talk have been published in the *Revolutionary Worker* newspaper in issues #1250-52, 1254-55, 1257-58 and 1260.

thing that's settled once and for all—the more solid core we get, in every situation, on every level, the more elasticity we should have. Can't have a solid core that has no elasticity within it. The core can't be so strong that everything is like a black hole and sucks in the light.

It is hard to do both sides of that. Look at this aspect of having the material force to defeat and then set the terms. This is like the movie *Remember the Titans*—the decision was made to integrate the high school in Virginia and the football team, and that the football coach was gonna be Black. Then they struggled things out from there. It provided better terms than simply saying, "do you want this integration"—a lot of white people would have said "no!" If you have the ability to set the terms, it's more favorable. "No, in socialist society you can't have religion taught in schools—if you want to, you can talk to your kids about that on your own time. But they're gonna come to the public school and learn science and history and a true approach to reality." How does that fit in with Catholics who can't be happy without the pope? There's no Catholicism without the pope. And that's a big contradiction. These are difficult contradictions, but we won't have a chance if we're not on this road. I wasn't being insincere in the talk on the dictatorship of the proletariat[10] in saying some of these ideas I'm bringing forward are, at this point, posing contradictions and indicating an approach, not attempting at this point to give a complete answer to all these things. But this is the way I am convinced we have to go about this whole thing we are doing. Both because it takes us where we want to go and because it's in line with our final goal of communism.

Engels' *Anti-Duhring* is very open about the fact that much of what was understood then would be surpassed and replaced by further understanding. This is the right orientation and approach—it is dialectical as well as materialist, it is not religious. The stuff from Newton is true on one level, but there's a larger reality he didn't grasp. This applies to us—there are many things that we don't understand, many things that will be discovered later that will surpass and replace some things we think are true now—but you have to go on this road to get there. It's a road with many divergent paths. How do you keep them all going in a good direction without being tightly in formation? The more you grasp that this is correct, the more you can have the solid core which enables you to do these things. This is about whether our communist

---

10. This refers to the talk *Dictatorship and Democracy, and the Socialist Transition to Communism*, mentioned above.

project is going to have any viability and desirability, and on the positive side it is opening up further pathways to solving these contradictions, and providing a path for others.

Those are the roads and that's how I see it—are we gonna get on this road, or not? Is this right what I'm saying? Is this how we should envision what we're all about? Or is it unrealistic, idealistic, nothing to do with the real world, not what we should aim for, not try to get there—are the people right who say "you want to do this, but you can't"? Not only can we, it is the only way we can do what we need to do. You can't repeat the experience [of the proletarian revolution and socialist society]. You couldn't do the Paris Commune again to do the Soviet Union. Too much has gone on, even besides the propaganda of the bourgeoisie, people are not going to get inspired to do the same thing. They should recognize that in its time and place the inspiration was the main thing. The Chinese revolution was much better than what they had before and much better than what they have now in China. But it's not enough to inspire people to do that again. And they shouldn't want to. Is what I'm arguing for a bunch of idealism? Or is it the only way we can go forward? What's the truth of this?

Objective and Partisan: Getting at the Truth

B.A. continues: Some of this in Feigon book on Mao[11] where Mao talks to his niece on reading the Bible—responding to her question about how to "inoculate" herself against it: "just go deeply into it and you'll come out the other side." Mao had some of this approach too, mixed in with other stuff. This has been there as an element: Mao had this aspect of not fearing to delve into things and seeking out the truth—perhaps he had this even more than Lenin—but then there's still a question of "political truth" or "class truth" getting in the way of this. In the name of the masses—and even out of concern for the masses. Mao had great concern for the masses, but these things were contending in Mao too. "You don't need any inoculation! Just go read it, you'll come out the other side." [There are] definitely correct things like that with Mao, but then there's also some "proletarian class truth," if not in the most narrow Stalinesque Lysenko way.[12]

A comrade: What about objective and partisan [that the outlook

---

11. Lee Feigon, *Mao, a Reinterpretation* (Chicago: Ivan R. Dee Publishers, 2002).

12. See "The Struggle in the Realm of Ideas," in this volume.

of the proletariat, of communists, is objective and partisan]?

B.A.: We should be able to get at the truth better than anybody. Our approach is not partisan in a utilitarian sense. We have an outlook and method that corresponds to a class that's emerged in history in the broadest sense, and it can't get itself out of this without overcoming all this stuff and transforming it all. This outlook corresponds to the proletariat's interests, but not narrowly.

I'm reading this book on Iran and Mossadegh [*All the Shah's Men*, by Stephen Kinzer].[13] Most of the newspapers [in Iran at that time] were controlled by the CIA, they had this political mobilization to oppose Mossadegh, and with all these attacks on him, he did not move to suppress any of this. And I said, "what the fuck have I set us up for with this solid core and elasticity?!" [*laughs*] That's why you don't let go of the solid core, and why we're different than Mossadegh.

The example of Brzezinski: On the tradition of autocracy in the Russian communist movement. I answered him, and said that the Russian Revolution negated all that.[14] But when I thought about that more, I said that's not a complete answer—he has a point here, and we have to acknowledge that the autocratic tradition seeped into the communist movement in some ways. I spoke to this in *Two Great Humps*.[15]

---

13. Stephen Kinzer, *All the Shah's Men: An American Coup and the Roots of Middle East Terror* (Hoboken, NJ: John Wiley & Sons, Inc., 2003). Mossadegh was the head of a popular and popularly elected government in Iran, who was overthrown by the U.S. government in 1953 through a CIA-led coup, working with and directing reactionary forces in Iran, and then putting the Shah on the throne as the ruler of Iran. The rule of the Shah, backed by and serving U.S. imperialism, led to widespread popular opposition but also strengthened the hand of reactionary fundamentalist Islamic forces in Iran, and in the late 1970s a popular uprising led to the overthrow of the Shah but unfortunately also to the rule of these reactionary religious fundamentalists.

14. Avakian, *Phony Communism Is Dead...Long Live Real Communism!*, 2nd edition (Chicago: RCP Publications, 2004), pp. 55-74.

15. *Getting Over the Two Great Humps: Further Thoughts on Conquering the World* is a talk given by Bob Avakian in the late 1990s. Excerpts from this talk appeared in the *Revolutionary Worker* and are available online at revcom.us. The series "On Proletarian Democracy and Proletarian Dictatorship – A Radically Different View of Leading Society" appeared in *RW* #1214 through 1226 (October 5, 2003-January 25, 2004). The series "Getting Over the Hump" appeared in *RW* #927, 930, 932, and 936-940 (October 12, November 2, November 16, and December 14, 1997 through January 18, 1998). Two additional excerpts from this talk are "Materialism and Romanticism: Can We Do Without Myth" in *RW* #1211 (August 24, 2003) and "Re-reading George Jackson" in *RW* #968 (August 9, 1998). All of these articles can be found online at revcom.us.

It is not "a clever device" when I say that reactionaries should be allowed to publish some books in socialist society—it is *good* to have these people interrogating us because we learn more about reality. It's part of how we're gonna learn and how the masses are gonna learn. It's tricky—flying universities and misogynist hip-hop. [Another comrade in the discussion had raised earlier the examples of how hip-hop had emerged from the masses and was contradictory, and the example of the "flying universities" in Poland during the '70s, which contained anti-regime lines and were suppressed.] If all you do is mobilize the masses to crush this, it's the same as state repression in other forms. You can't let misogyny run rampant and not challenge it and not suppress it in certain ways—but on the other hand, even just coming up with ways that masses oppose this is not always the way to do this. Flying universities—what to do? Let them go on in a certain way? Or shut them down? We have to know what they're doing. You can't be Mossadegh, you need a political police—you need to know about plots, real plots that will go on, to overthrow socialism—but you shouldn't rely on state repression as the way to deal with opposition in every form, and sometimes you don't even want your own people to go into these things, because then it's not really a free university because you've got your people in there and it can be chilling, so we have to think about it. But if we don't have a lot of people proceeding from this outlook and methodology and applying themselves to this, people who have deeply internalized this kind of outlook, method and approach, we'll never be able to handle it right. This is a different vision—it's different than even the best of the GPCR—there is the other dimension that we need of ferment in society as I've been speaking about it, a different, an additional dimension to ferment in society, including intellectual ferment. This is not alien to Mao, but he didn't develop this into a whole strategic approach.

In the Feigon book, he says Mao came up inside of the Soviet model, so to speak, and then Mao said no, we gotta break out of this whole way of building socialism. Mao was the first attempt in this. Then there is a whole other dimension as a strategic approach that incorporates things from the GPCR. It was and has been for a long time and acutely something I've had to fight for. What I'm calling for is really hard to do, but it's the only way we can really do this. In the future, people will go further with everything that's involved in getting to communism; but at this point, this is what we have to go through.

Even the best of the GPCR posed against this turns into its opposite. Revolution develops through stages and people get stuck—and things turn into their opposites and what's advanced doesn't remain advanced when there are new necessities posed that you have to break through on.

This approach will involve a tremendous struggle with the masses. When speaking to that professor's question [how would you do better than in the Soviet Union and in China] I had to speak to this: there are masses who have been lorded over by people who know more than they do, and they're not gonna want to listen under socialism to people saying the new society is no good. I said: I don't believe in tailing people just because they've been oppressed. They're gonna be leading society and we have to struggle with them over what this is all about. In order to do this, people have to understand how to make the distinction between voicing reactionary opinions and actively working to overthrow the whole socialist system; and even more fundamentally they have to know *why* it is important to make that distinction. He asked this question so I explored it as best I could. Because this is something that adds a whole strategic dimension and embodies but goes further than the GPCR; and if, in the name of upholding the GPCR, you resist the part that goes further—then you're opposing the whole thing.

It's a tricky contradiction that, on the one hand, we have to always go for the truth—and not for "political truth" or "class truth"—and, on the other hand, we have to know how to lead without giving up the core. In taking all this up, some people are veering to social-democracy and others refuse to recognize there's any problem here and don't even want to criticize Stalin. And in this situation, you can convince yourself that if you criticize Stalin then you have someone to the left of you and someone to the right and then you must be correct(!)—as opposed to whether you're correct or not is based on whether it's true.

Objective and partisan is like this: If it's true, it should be part of advancing, getting us where we're going. If it's not true, it would get in the way. If it's true, even if it reveals the ugliest side of what we're about—if that black book thing were true we'd have to say how did that happen and how do we prevent that?—but the thing is, what matters is that whatever is true, we can encompass it and make it part of what we're all about, even when it's truths that reveal bad aspects of what we've done. [The "black book" refers to a book purporting to tell the "true story of communism"—and to attack it as a monstrous crime—it is a combination of slanders and lies mixed in with some references to actual shortcomings and errors in the experience of socialist society so far.[16]]

That's the synthesis of partisan and objective. Either we actually believe the most fundamental truth about capitalism and communism is what it is—either we have a scientifically grounded understanding of why communism should and can replace capitalism, all over the world—or we don't, in which case we end up fearing truth.

We have to rupture more fully with instrumentalism—with notions of making reality an "instrument" of our objectives, of distorting reality to try to make it serve our ends, of "political truth." The dynamic of "truths that make us cringe" is part of what can be driving us forward. This can help call forth that ferment so that we can understand reality. This is scientific materialist objectivity. If you go deeply enough and understand that these contradictions now posed could lead to a different era based on the resolution of those contradictions, then you want to set in motion a dynamic where people *are* bringing out your shortcomings. Not that every mistake should be brought out in a way to overwhelm everything we're trying to do, but in a strategic sense [we should] welcome this and not try to manage it too much—you *want* that, the back and forth. On the web, there have been slanders and outright pig-type stuff in relation to me, which doesn't do any good for anybody trying to do good in the world, and this kind of harmful stuff should not be tolerated by anybody who does want to do good in the world. But there has also been political debate about my role as a leader and about communist leaders in general. This has generally been fairly low-level, but at least it has had some substance, and is it bad to have this kind of debate not only now but also under socialism? No, *this* is a good thing. Not only because people will be able to learn more in general, but *we'll* be able to learn more. What is coming forward? What are the ways that we have to go forward? What is the baggage that we have to cast off? If you get the epistemology, you really want this. This is not just a tactical, but a *strategic* view flowing from this epistemological view of what this process should be—and we'll get where we need to go with this ferment. Not just tolerating this, but being enthusiastic—not about everything insulting, but generally. Do we think this is a good process, not only now but under the dictatorship of the proletariat? Or should we just stick with the seemingly safer path of what we've done before?

---

16. Stephane Courtois, et al., *The Black Book of Communism: Crimes, Terror, Repression* (Cambridge: Harvard University Press, 1999).

I'm talking about a new synthesis—a more thoroughly materialist epistemology. Lenin wrote *Materialism and Empirio-Criticism* where he argued against these things [like "political truth," or "truth as an organizing principle"] but sometimes the practical Lenin got in the way of the philosophical Lenin. The political exigencies that were imposed contributed to a situation where some of the way Lenin dealt with contradictions had an aspect of Stalin. There are many examples of this in *The Furies* [a book on the French and Russian revolutions by Arno Mayer].[17] In some instances, the Bolsheviks had a kind of "Mafia" approach in some areas, especially during the civil war that followed the October 1917 Revolution. In some cases, when people would be organized by reactionaries to fight against the Bolsheviks, the Bolsheviks would retaliate broadly and without mercy. Or they would kill people not only for deserting the Red Army but even for dragging their feet in fighting the civil war. While sometimes in the midst of war, extreme measures may be necessary, overall this is not the way to deal with these contradictions. I addressed some of this in *Two Great Humps*—I read Lenin on this and thought, "this is not right." There's epistemological stuff bound up with all this as well.

We Communists Stand for Truth

B.A. continues: I'm trying to set a framework for the whole approach to our project. Who's right: me, or people who say you can't avoid doing things the way that people have done it up to now? Some even say: "I wish you could, but I don't think you can." Is what I'm arguing for really a materialist way of approaching our project? Is this really what we have to go through now to get where we need to go? Is this, analogically, Einstein to Newton, or is it a bunch of nonsense— since Newtonian physics can describe the reality around us and has empirical evidence on its side? Is there in fact no other way to do what I'm arguing for, no other way to get to communism? Or is the other road really the reality of it?

Is what I'm arguing for just, at best, some interesting and intriguing ideas and provocative thinking—or is it really the way we have to approach things, as I've said?

Even more fundamentally, having to do with my point on communists having the most trouble admitting their mistakes—which has

---

17. Arno J. Mayer, *The Furies: Violence and Terror in the French and Russian Revolutions* (Princeton, NJ: Princeton University Press, 2000).

to do with no one else is trying to remake the world—but is it even important for us to try to get to the truth of things?[18] Or are we politicians who are trying to achieve certain political objectives, and all that other stuff about getting to the truth is a bunch of petty bourgeois nonsense, since we're about "getting to power"? It's a fundamental question of two roads here. One of the big questions is "are we really people who are trying to get to the truth, or is it really just a matter of 'truth as an organizing principle'?" Lenin criticized this philosophically—"truth as an organizing principle"—and you can criticize it to reject religion and opportunism which you don't find particularly useful, but you can end up doing this yourself in another form. Mao said we communists stand for truth—we should be scientific and honest. Is this a concern of ours? Or is our concern to just know enough truth to accomplish our objectives as we perceive them at a given time? Just enough truth to accomplish our objectives—even if we apply this not on the most narrow level and instead our approach is that the truth we need is what we need to get to the "four alls." [The "four alls" refers to the achievement of the necessary conditions for communism. It refers to a statement by Marx that the dictatorship of the proletariat is the necessary transition to the abolition of all class distinctions, of all the production relations on which these class distinctions rest, of all the social relations that correspond to these production relations, and to the revolutionizing of all the ideas that correspond to these relations.[19]]

* * * * *

A second comrade: Fundamental answer is that we're part of material reality and our stage or canvas is matter in motion—that's what we're trying to work with, work on. There is no such thing as determinate human nature. We are trying to transform things.

The question of falsifiability. This is a big critique of Marxism from the outside—that Marxism is not really a science, Marxists are not rigorous and don't follow scientific methods. One of the criteria of real science is that it's inherently falsifiable. Lot of confusion about what that means. Example of Karl Popper: Marxism is not really a science but

---

18. See "Moving Towards Communism," *Revolutionary Worker* #1260 (November 28, 2004), from *Dictatorship and Democracy, and the Socialist Transition to Communism*. The full text is available online at revcom.us.

19. For a fuller discussion of this see the talk by Bob Avakian, *Dictatorship and Democracy, and the Socialist Transition to Communism*.

a faith. [Stephen Jay] Gould's point on evolution as a fact. Is the theory of evolution inherently falsifiable? Yes. If you came up with something that challenged the whole framework, it would collapse. One of the strengths of evolution is that it's been open to falsification for a long time now but no one has been able to do it.

We communists have some foundational assumptions about the fundamental contradiction [of capitalism], etc. which are solidly established, but that doesn't mean that there's a lot that isn't going to change and evolve. Human knowledge develops and matter is never static. If we're dealing with matter in motion, there's a lot to learn—whatever field you're studying. There's a tremendous amount of cross-fertilization between different spheres of science and knowledge. If you're looking at it [communism] as not being a religious faith, but a science, the truth matters for that. If we're trying to transform things, then we can't do it without a grasp of the truth. The only way we couldn't be concerned with the truth is if we want it to be a religion, or just reduce communism to a sort of code of ethics.

Is our thing a science? Very different than some code in the name of the masses.

A lot of people think that the reason for the evolution series[20] was an offensive by the Christian fascists against evolution. That was one reason—but on the other hand it is important for the communists and the masses to be trained in a basic understanding of how the life of the planet evolved.

This narrow-mindedness would be the death of us. It matters a lot that people understand the basic laws and so on of the transformation of matter.

B.A.: A lot of the things I've been struggling for in terms of methods of leadership is [against the notion] that when you get down to reality you can't do things this way. Partly because this is very messy. This is turbulent. To somehow open the gate to the truth is letting the sharks into the water. Well, we have our criticisms of Stalin and other people have theirs, and there is the reality of Lenin's statement that it takes ten pages of truth to answer one sentence of opportunism—that's

---

20. Ardea Skybreak's series *The Science of Evolution* appeared in the *Revolutionary Worker* #1157, 1159-1160, 1163-1164, 1170, 1179-1183, and 1215-1223 (June 30, July 21-28, August 18-25, October 6, December 15, 2002-January 19, 2003 and October 12-December 21, 2004).

gonna be true in the world for a long time. You don't always have ten pages that you can devote to answer a sentence of bullshit—you're at a disadvantage. People can pick out something and divorce it from the larger reality from which it arises. In China people went hungry and starved in the Great Leap Forward—but what's the larger context? Our enemies don't have to be materialist or dialectical and go into the reality and contradictions and necessity. We have an orientation of grasping what they were up against and then talking about how to do better in the context of that kind of reality. Other people won't do that. They'll come from their own class viewpoints—often ignorance combined with arrogance to make pronouncements. This is messy. It isn't like we're all just talking in the realm of a bunch of scientists about evolution and what's true—creationists are not interested in getting at the truth. Other people have their own agendas and their own "political truths"—so to say "knock down the breakwater, let the sharks get in" makes things messy. So then the question is, is that really a better way to do it? Or should we swim behind the breakwater and head straight for the shore, keep your arms inside the boat. And there *are* sharks out there.

So methodologically and epistemologically and ideologically this is a question of what I'm fighting for versus the thing of "you can't do it that way." "It's not what we're about and we can't do it this way." Are we a bunch of instrumentalists? Do we want just enough truth so we can navigate narrowly to some notion of where we need to go?—which will end up the wrong place. Because your boat will get turned around with the wrong course. Philosophically you can't do it that way—you can't navigate reality that way to get to where you need to go. It's not the way reality is. We can't get there that way—and the "there" will not be the there that we want. That's the only communism there'll be—not a kingdom of great harmony, but turbulent. And for the same reason that's what I'm struggling for. If you don't see that, then you become what I fear our movement has been way too much: "why would we want to concern ourselves with that?"

The reason I'm raising this dimension is that it relates to the stereotype—but not simply the stereotype—of what we communists have been like. Right now I'm wrestling with Rawls' *Theory of Justice*. He insists that you cannot justify things on the basis that they serve the larger social good if it tramples on the needs and rights of individuals—if you proceed down that road you get to totalitarianism.

To me that's wrong—founded on idealism, not on a real, materialist understanding of society. But we have to wrestle with that, as in

GO&GS on the individual and the collective.[21] There's more work to be done even in that sphere—not trampling on individuals just because it's in the interests of society as a whole.

In reply to those who attack Mao for sending intellectuals to the countryside, there is the correct point of, "look, nobody in China asked the peasants if *they* wanted to be in the countryside"—a very important point, but if that's the end of it, or the only point, you're back to what we've been too much. This is parallel to whether the truth should matter to us.

A third comrade: [In regard to] method and approach and sharks in choppy water. There is a lot of stuff out there which is not encompassed in our understanding at this point. And it often seems to present itself as irrelevant, a distraction, or a refutation of our understanding. And there is a question of fundamental orientation epistemologically. To how one is looking at that. And your [Chairman Avakian's] concept is attacking a lot of barriers to that. That is welcome. Look at the analysis of the 1980s. [This refers to the RCP's analysis that, during that period, there would be the outbreak of world war between the imperialist bloc headed by the U.S. and that headed by the Soviet Union, unless this world war were prevented by revolution in large and/or strategic enough areas of the world.] There is your insistence on examining what it was that we did [in terms of that analysis]. Or the self-criticism you [referring to Chairman Avakian] have made about underestimating the "information technology revolution" and [having missed] the relevance of that. [This refers to a self-critical observation by Chairman Avakian that in his book *For a Harvest of Dragons*, written in the early 1980s, that he was too dismissive of comments by revisionist leaders of the Soviet Union at that time about the great changes that were being brought about by the "information revolution."] Here was something coming from Soviet revisionists! But [though seeming] irrelevant, in one context, all these different levels of reality are aspects of reality. Ignore them at your peril. There is a lot of resistance [to this approach] but the masses need to understand the world in all its dimensions. Mankind consciously transforming itself. It has to do with transforming all of material reality....What is communism? And where

---

21. *Great Objectives and Grand Strategy* (*GO&GS*) is a talk by Bob Avakian at the end of the 1990s; excerpts from it have been published in the *Revolutionary Worker* #1127-1142 (November 18, 2001 through March 10, 2002). They are available online at revcom.us.

do things go from there? Has to do with getting there. A materialist understanding of the world and the relation of humanity to it. We can't get there if you are picking the parts of reality which seem to matter. Marching along an economist and revisionist road, those other aspects of reality are unwelcome intrusions into that. It matters to understand material reality if you are really a communist and a materialist. To really understand Marxist economics, to comprehend the world now, to accurately reflect material reality.

A fourth comrade: On this question of the sharks. The heart of the question is can we handle the sharks. Can we handle the problems? If we can do it then why couldn't the masses? I remember a discussion of "End of a Stage/Beginning of a New Stage,"[22] where the tilt was: how much can we keep of Stalin? There was a lot of bad shit that happened under Stalin, and there were problems in the GPCR too. We have to look at that. You can't do it unless you sit in that "godlike position of the proletariat." But religious faith keeps us from looking at that. I came to that Nat Turner place on this: This is the slaves making history. We have to look at this in that light. It is valid for slaves to end slavery. People get uptight about looking at these things, but we will have to deal with this....If we can't take this on now, how can we take it on when we have state power?

In the *Reaching/Flying* series, in the last installment, it says there are two things we don't know how to do.[23] We don't yet know how to actually defeat the other side and seize power when the time comes, and we don't yet know how to actually withstand the much heavier repression that is coming. This is heavy. Is this the right way to go about things? Here's this idea that we can put this out to the masses. Is that the way to go? The solid core/elasticity dialectic. Can we withstand all this? People are going to do things in practice that you aren't going to have under your control. Is this the way to learn about and transform the world? Why do we need a poetic spirit, as the Chair has said? Why is it dangerous not to have one, and how is it related to an unsatiable desire to know about and transform the world? Do you need the per-

22. Avakian, "The End of a Stage—The Beginning of a New Stage" (late 1989), in *Revolution*, No. 60 (Fall 1990).

23. "Conclusion: The Challenges We Must Take Up," *Revolutionary Worker* #1210 (August 17, 2003). This is from the series *Reaching for the Heights and Flying Without a Safety Net*, a talk by Bob Avakian toward the end of 2002; excerpts from it appeared in the *RW* #1195-1210 (April 20-August 17, 2003), available online at revcom.us.

spective of the "godlike position of the proletariat" and your [Chairman Avakian's] earlier point on looking at the parade of humanity walking by? If you don't do that, it's sentimental—phony emotionalism as opposed to a grasp that the potential of people is what is being held back and chained in by this system.

I have often wondered about why the second to the last paragraph in *Harvest of Dragons* says what it does. ["In the final analysis, as Engels once expressed it, the proletariat must win its emancipation on the battlefield. But there is not only the question of winning in this sense but of how we win in the largest sense. One of the significant if perhaps subtle and often little-noticed ways in which the enemy, even in defeat, seeks to exact revenge on the revolution and sow the seed of its future undoing is in what he would force the revolutionaries to become in order to defeat him. It will come to this: we will have to face him in the trenches and defeat him amidst terrible destruction but we must not in the process annihilate the fundamental difference between the enemy and ourselves. Here the example of Marx is illuminating: he repeatedly fought at close quarters with the ideologists and apologists of the bourgeoisie but he never fought them on their terms or with their outlook; with Marx his method is as exhilarating as his goal is inspiring. We must be able to maintain our firmness of principles but at the same time our flexibility, our materialism and our dialectics, our realism and our romanticism, our solemn sense of purpose and our sense of humor."][24] Why would that be in there if it hasn't come to that? This is what the Chair "models" and challenges us on. That is not something off to the side of what we are doing, but integral to what we're doing.

Embrace But Not Replace: Sharks and Guppies

B.A.: I have been reading this interview with Chomsky and Barsamian. At one point Barsamian says, I won't ask you what your politics has to do with your linguistics, and Chomsky says thanks. He sees them as completely separate, and he's been assaulted with an instrumentalist view—i.e., that the two should "have something to do with each other," in a mechanical sense. No doubt, there *is* a connection, but it's on a whole other level and not in some mechanical, reductionist, one-to-one sense.

In another discussion, speaking of human beings' capabilities

---

24. Avakian, *For a Harvest of Dragons: On the "Crisis of Marxism" and the Power of Marxism—Now More Than Ever* (Chicago: RCP Publications, 1983), p. 152.

with language, Chomsky asks whether we can conclude that the human competence for language is a product of evolution. Yes, he answers, but we can't say exactly how. Well, obviously, the point is not to leave it there, more will have to be learned scientifically about all this. But is this work on how humans acquire knowledge important to us? Yes.

What's involved is somewhat like doing art in a certain way. Here again we could say there are three models: First, the classical CP trade-unionist economist approach of get the artists on the picket lines.[25] Second, let the artists be cogs and wheels in the machinery of the revolution. Or let them do art that serves the revolution, even if not in a narrow sense. Yes, let them do art that serves the revolution; but besides "model works"—which they developed in the Cultural Revolution in China and around which we also need to do better, and which require attention—we also need a third approach, or model: artists doing their art that does not narrowly serve things. When I raised these contradictions with one artist—how would artists create art in a new society and yet not lose their connection with other artists, and with the masses of people—he raised the idea of artists living and working in cooperatives and, besides their art, also doing some things to contribute to society in other ways. This is worth thinking about, as one dimension of things. And of course people are going to have to get funded and the funders are going to have to combine funding for things that directly serve the revolution and things that do not directly serve it.

There's a role for people going off and you don't know what it's gonna lead to. We need art that directly relates to the struggle, art that is like the model works, and art where the artists go off and follow their impulse. That dimension in the arts and sciences—with that process going on of people being funded with a general idea of what they want to explore and you don't conclude it's wasted if sometimes they don't come up with anything. You have to recognize that part of the process is that some of this won't lead to anything. This actually relates to Lenin's point on communism springing from every pore of society, understood in the broadest sense. Yes [a young comrade who is studying science] should wage struggle regarding philosophy of science, and should struggle for MLM, including as a means to get more compre-

---

25. This was a shorthand way of describing the orientation of the CPUSA which was marked by a utilitarian and instrumentalist approach to art—focusing the attention of artists on the workers movement in a narrow way, reification of the proletariat in art, and a view of art, and reality, that never really broke with radical democracy to embrace the two radical ruptures described by Marx.

hensively to the truth. But it's also true that if someone discovers something about what happened the day before the Big Bang it is (a) interesting to know, and (b) not in a narrow way becomes part of the revolutionary process and the class struggle. Different classes will interpret things in different ways and seek to suppress things in different ways. (It's not just the proletariat that has sometimes sought to suppress science for political and ideological reasons—look at what Bush, et. al., are doing right now!!)

Look, the world actually is made up of matter in motion, and materialism and dialectics does correspond to the way the world is and enables us to get more deeply to it. And therefore, discovering more about reality can be encompassed by and actually strengthens dialectical materialism; and when there are classes struggling over this, it becomes part of the class struggle in the ideological realm. The pursuit of knowledge should not be reduced to discovering things in order to wage struggle in the ideological realm, but the way it works is that you learn more about reality and if you correctly understand dialectical materialism whatever is learned, whatever truths are discovered, will reinforce, strengthen and enrich dialectical materialism and will inevitably become part of the class struggle—and even under communism part of the ideological struggle. Yes, part of it for that young comrade is waging the class struggle in that realm [of science and philosophy of science], but it's not limited to or reduced to that.

The second comrade: This gets back to how are we training people to think. What kind of people do we want to be in terms of fitting ourselves to rule? We talk about the masses searching for philosophy, [but] are *we* searching for philosophy? The Chair is trying to push the limits. The opposing approach it that "we have our kit," and he keeps upsetting that. How are we going to answer the questions posed by various intellectuals on whether we can really wield state power in this way? How are you going to handle this or that? Too often communists give facile answers. They rule things out of order and that gives rise to Orwells. Some questions come from the wrong place, but you can't determine that *a priori*. The waters are choppy, and there are sharks, but it turns out a lot are toothless guppies. We have to train people including in relation to contradictions among the people. A sweeping view of "embraces but does not replace" means we look to learning from all these spheres. ["Embraces but does not replace" refers to a principle formulated by Mao Tsetung that Marxism embraces but does not replace theories in physics, the arts, etc. This has been further developed and applied by Bob Avakian.[26]] There is struggle over how the world actually develops: in a gradual way or through punctuations. Does this matter to us? How the universe is? It matters to how matter is in motion. We are part of matter. There are some principles underlying all matter in motion. And we need to understand these things through the sciences and arts [with] the correct approach, and not ruling things out of order. In the Soviet Union people were suppressed wrongly in relation to this. If this wrong line gets into power, this will happen. There is this point to the toothless guppies. But we can't tell the difference between sharks and toothless guppies if we don't go for the truth of things. There are a lot of ways the truth matters. Why were people shocked by statements by you [referring to Chairman Avakian] that not just in terms of our party but historically there has been a problem in the communist movement—that most of the time most communists are not communists!—and that if we don't rupture with certain things, then we won't be able to seize power—or do anything good with it if somehow we did seize power? If people are steeped in materialism, they would not be shocked by this and would be able to deal with this. We're not going to be able to manage and control the truth. It springs forward from matter. The truth is not scary.

B.A.: All that is very important. At the same time, if we don't understand what we are trying to take on with this method and approach I'm struggling for—if we don't grasp the principles involved in "solid core with a lot of elasticity" and related things—we will be drawn and quartered. It is going to be messy and difficult. It is going to be messy. It is also going to be exhilarating. It is going to mean that we really have to be communists and apply this on the highest level. I want to make very clear that if this other kind of line holds sway and people come to power with that line, it is going to be very bad. You are right that strategically this is not frightening. I agree with the basic thrust of your comments, but maybe there is a secondary aspect in which this is a bit frightening. We shouldn't underestimate the difficulties. Within this is going to be a lot of tumult. The argument that you can't do this [the way I am proposing] is not without any basis in material reality.

But the more powerful material reality is that this can be done— this method and approach of solid core with a lot of elasticity, as I have been developing and fighting for it, can be carried out—and in fact this is the only way to do it, the only way we can get to communism.

---

26. See, for example, his discussion of this in *Dictatorship and Democracy, and the Socialist Transition to Communism*.

MARXISM IS A SCIENCE,
IT IS NOT "THE END OF PHILOSOPHY"

Engels said (in *Anti-Duhring*): With scientific socialism [Marxism] all that's left of philosophy is dialectics and formal logic. I don't think that's right. I believe the principle that Marxism "embraces but does not replace"[1] particular spheres of human knowledge and endeavor applies to the realm of philosophy too. What about someone like Derrida (a French "post-modernist," "deconstructionist" philosopher, who recently died but has had a large influence not only in Europe, and elsewhere, but among some intellectuals in the U.S.)? Is there anything to learn from him? Bill Martin has a lot of regard for Derrida.[2] He [Martin] has a fair amount where he doesn't agree with us, as well as a lot of unity. But is there anything to engage about shortcomings he sees in Marxism? Yes, definitely.

I believe it's a mistake to say that Marxism has put an end to philosophy. Philosophy "in its own right," and not just Marxist philosophy, narrowly conceived, can still teach us things. "Embraces, but does not

---

1. "Embraces but does not replace" refers to a principle formulated by Mao Tsetung that Marxism embraces but does not replace the various spheres of science and art, and other realms of human thought and endeavor. This concept has been further developed and applied by Bob Avakian. See, for example, his discussion of this in *Dictatorship and Democracy, and the Socialist Transition to Communism* (available on the web at revcom.us) and "Marxism 'Embraces But Does Not Replace,'" which appears in this volume.

2. Bill Martin is a social theorist and professor of philosophy at DePaul University, Chicago. He is the co-author, with Bob Avakian, of *Marxism and the Call of the Future: Conversations on Ethics, History, and Politics* (Chicago: Open Court, 2005). His numerous books also include: *Politics in the Impasse* (1996), *The Radical Project: Sartrean Investigations* (2001), and *Avant Rock* (2002).

replace" applies here too. What about questions of being and existence and the meaning of human existence? What about someone like Heidegger (a very influential German "existentialist" philosopher)? There was a point in our conversation when I reminded Bill Martin of something I had read where he said that he gets angry when people insist that you can ignore, or dismiss, Heidegger's philosophy because Heidegger became a supporter of the Nazis. I told Bill I agreed with him on that—you still have to evaluate Heidegger's philosophy as such, as philosophy. I also said to Bill: I *do* think that it is correct to discuss what there is about Heidegger's philosophy that would lead him to support the Nazis, but we have to engage it.

We need lots of people doing this, and we need to recruit into our party many people who know something about these spheres—we can no longer have people thinking this is all a waste of time. "Why are you reading Derrida?—that's a waste of time." We cannot have that kind of attitude any more. This is part of the dialogue. Of course, a lot of petty bourgeois outlooks get expressed by various people in all these kinds of exchanges—so what? I said to Bill Martin: There is no "transcendental meaning" to human existence—nothing beyond the realm of human experience to give it meaning—the only meaning is what is given to existence by humans. And Bill answered: "Amen." We both laughed. This was a good exchange.

We need lots of people doing that. There is no notion in the dialogue with Bill Martin that I am coming from something other than an MLM framework. But you have to actually engage what other people are raising—and not simply, crudely respond to everything they say with: "Let me reinterpret that in MLM terms." If you see MLM as a science, and not a religion, you can handle this correctly.

Now, it is true, if we don't seize power, we can't really give full expression to all this. We do have to seize power—we do have to keep our eye on that prize—or this becomes an exercise in itself. We need to keep re-engaging and wrangling with that question. *But* we also need to not lose sight of what power is for. This is the question of "winning...and winning": We are not just out to seize power for its own sake, but to transform things with power—and to do it with a vision of a whole different world.

It isn't only with the intellectuals that this is a good approach. We have to engage masses of people, we have to learn from them—and, yes, we have to struggle with them. Even after people, including from the basic masses, are recruited into the party, this process should go on—

although now in a different way. People have a wealth of experience and a lot of thinking—some of it is correct and some incorrect. There is still a question not only of how to develop unity with people when they are *not* communists but also how to continue bringing people forward when they *are* communists—and there is the question of how to struggle with them even after they make the leap to being communists.

Lots of people can become communists and approach things this way. The point is, you have to get with this method and approach to do this—and, if they take this up and go with it, lots of people can do lots of good things, working and struggling in a good way with all kinds of people.

INTOXICATED WITH THE TRUTH

In reading what I have said recently about epistemology (theory of knowledge) some people, including some who consider themselves communists, have commented, and not entirely in a positive way in all cases: "It seems you are intoxicated with the truth." Alright, I'm intoxicated with truth—yes, I'm not ashamed to say that. The big bang—discovering more about that—isn't that worthwhile and exciting?

There is a whole part in the epistemology discussion I had with some comrades[1] about how truth becomes part of the struggle for communism. What is the relation between objective and partisan—how should we correctly understand that Marxism is *both* partisan *and* objective? Anyone who thinks it's not important to actually know the truth will do a lot of harm. And anyone who thinks it's *just* a matter of seeking the truth misses how this should be unfolded. Truths do not exist in a vacuum. Truths that are discovered enter into a whole process by which we are better able to know and change the world. But not in a narrow and utilitarian way. With a utilitarian outlook there is a whole dimension being missed. This has to do with how people see the concept of "solid core with a lot of elasticity."[2] Those who have a narrow

---

1. See "Bob Avakian in a Discussion with Comrades on Epistemology: On Knowing and Changing the World," in this volume.

2. Avakian discusses this concept in the talk *Dictatorship and Democracy, and the Socialist Transition to Communism* as follows: "[Y]ou have to have a solid core that firmly grasps and is committed to the strategic objectives and aims and process of the struggle for communism. If you let go of that you are just giving everything back to the capitalists in one form or another, with all the horrors that means. At the same time, if you don't allow for a lot of diversity and people running in all kinds of directions with things, then not only are people going to be building up tremendous resentment against you, but you are also not going to have the rich kind

68

and utilitarian approach don't understand why we need this process of struggling for the truth as part of the socialist transition to communism.

Truth *is* good for the proletariat. I don't mean that in a narrow way. Truth is good for the political struggle, yes—the more that is understood about reality, the more favorable it will be strategically for the proletariat and its revolutionary objectives. But there is a whole thing being missed if truth is approached in a narrow and utilitarian way. If somebody discovers something about the big bang, that will be interesting and exciting. Truths are important just for what they are, because that's the kind of world we want to get to. For what they are. Human beings do need to be amazed. You don't need religion to realize or appreciate that. In the motion of the material world and the inter-action of human beings with the rest of reality, mysteries get resolved and new mysteries emerge. Why wouldn't someone with broadness of mind be interested in questions of cosmology in their own right? (Cos-mology refers to the science and philosophy of the origins and devel-opment of the universe.) On the other hand, in another dimension, so long as society is divided into classes, anything that is learned will become part of the class struggle in many different ways, including in the dimension of the proletariat knowing the world more profoundly to change it more profoundly.

I was talking about this with someone the other day: one of the ironies is that you get people who are academics, intellectuals, etc., who become communists and then they often become narrow, "workerist" and philistine in regard to their own sphere of specialized knowledge. They denigrate their own sphere. They have a dualist attitude—they love it but they are guilt-ridden about loving it. This is the Menshe-vism[3]—the narrowness, the economism and philistinism—that has been the prevailing view in the communist movement—a tailing after the backwardness that the system has imposed on masses of people, a tailing which will lead ultimately to reinforcing capitalism and the

---

of process out of which the greatest truth and ability to transform reality will emerge." ("A World We Would Want to Live In," *Revolutionary Worker* #1257 [October 31, 2004].)

3. The term "Menshevism" is taken from the experience of the Russian revolu-tion, where those who wanted to reduce the socialist movement essentially to a struggle for reforms, often couched in the form of upholding the immediate inter-ests of the workers and tailing after their spontaneous views, came to be called "Mensheviks," in opposition to the revolutionary outlook and strategic approach of Lenin and his followers, the Bolsheviks.

oppressive and exploitative relations that characterize capitalist rule.

There was something wrong that was being promoted with that Goldbach conjecture guy obviously. [This refers to a mathematician in China who was working on a problem of mathematical theory known as the Goldbach conjecture; he was promoted by the revisionists, headed ultimately by Deng Xiaoping, after they seized power in China, following Mao's death in 1976.] It was part of a whole wrong line on the relation between science and transforming society. It was an idealist vision and a vision that would lead to what they have in China now—to the restoration of capitalism and extreme polarization in society, with masses of people sunk again into desperate poverty and oppression. But our response—what we brought forward was the Menshevik answer. In the context of polemicizing against the Mensheviks, we gave a Menshevik answer. That is why we had to criticize ourselves in this regard.[4] The point is that we gave the standard Menshevik view of those kinds of things. There has been a lot of this kind of thing—what we could call "Menshevik hackism"—in the communist movement, including our own party, and we need to rupture with it deeply and thoroughly. With that kind of outlook and approach you just can't have any real appreciation for science, or for art and culture.

Yes, I do think there is something to the point Bill Martin raised about poetic truth.[5] He raised that, in its own way, art contains or expresses truth. There is more to be explored there. I don't think what I said, in response to that, in the conversation with Bill Martin, is wrong, but I do believe there is more to be explored. Maybe what I said is not the whole of the truth about it either. These questions come up and you wrangle with them, and there is a finite limit to what you can do in a conversation like that. Then you have to revisit these questions at some point.

As much as I like [the English romantic poet of the early 19th

---

4. See "How the Mensheviks Take Revisionism as the Key Link," in *Revolution and Counter-revolution: The Revisionist Coup in China and the Struggle in the Revolutionary Communist Party, USA* (Chicago: RCP Publications, 1978), p. 280, and "The Correct Approach to Intellectuals...Engels Got Upset When Duhring Was Removed From His University Post," *Revolutionary Worker* No. 1226 (January 25, 2004), from *Getting Over the Two Great Humps: Further Thoughts on Conquering the World* by Bob Avakian.

5. This refers to a point raised by Bill Martin, in the conversation with Bob Avakian, which has been published as the book *Marxism and the Call of the Future: Conversations on Ethics, History, and Politics* (Chicago: Open Court Press, 2005).

century] Keats, I don't believe in the Keats line that "Beauty is truth, truth beauty..." But there is something about the role of beauty. Why do people need art? Is it simply a matter of the much misused Lenin quote about artists being cogs in the revolutionary machinery? And, by the way, that is not all Lenin thought about art, which is why I say "misused." We need more synthesis on these kinds of questions. Do human beings need play, do they need beauty? Do you have to be apologetic because you are a communist and you think something is worthwhile just because it is play? It doesn't have "the triumphal march of the proletariat," you know [laughs]. I don't think so. But that kind of thing has been a common, even prevalent, view among communists. Yes, sure, ultimately none of this escapes the realm of social content, and specifically class content in this world that is marked by profound class divisions. But you can't be reductionist about that.

Take Shakespeare, for example: there is definite class content to that. But there are some things that are not simply reducible to class content about Shakespeare. There is the use of language in Shakespeare that is not reducible simply to its class content. And there are questions of philosophy, and so on, that are still of interest. That is why it still resonates with people in different class societies, and even with us. You have to have a historical materialist attitude, not a Menshevik attitude, toward these things. That is the point in the broadest, most sweeping sense. Of course, all this can't escape social content. You should examine the social content, the class content of what Shakespeare is about. But that is not the end of the story about Shakespeare, or things from other eras. This is something we are discovering more about, I think—something we have to go back to and get a deeper synthesis on. There is more to be explored about these kinds of questions.

This doesn't mean we are throwing out our class viewpoint. It means we are coming to a better understanding of what that class viewpoint really means. Our class viewpoint is not Menshevik economism. It is historical materialism, dialectical materialism. That is our class viewpoint. Not Menshevik economist revengism with its narrow attitude toward the intellectuals and other strata.

This is very important. Otherwise, we will make a mess of things once again. There have been lots of messes made by people who at least claimed to be communists—messes that resulted in large part because they were not really communist in their outlook and their method.

We have to keep coming back to these things. We can't lose our grounding in why we need to bring forward the people, the proletarians and other basic masses, who have to be the backbone and driving force in this revolution, because there is materialism in that. Leibel Bergman was wrong: You can't make revolution with dentists. [Leibel Bergman, a former leader of the RCP, went from being a communist to supporting the reactionary coup in China after Mao's death and the restoration of capitalism there under Deng Xiaoping—see *From Ike To Mao...and Beyond: My Journey From Mainstream America to Revolutionary Communist, a Memoir by Bob Avakian*.] One time, Leibel said: "Well, we talk about the proletariat, but if we became convinced that dentists were the key force to make revolution, we would have to win dentists to Marxism-Leninism." I replied, "I don't think so." Obviously, he was choosing dentists deliberately to make a point. But nonetheless, there is a reason why we talk about how it is a *proletarian* revolution—a revolution in which the proletariat must be the backbone. It is not a revolution of good-hearted people with no social or class content. But we shouldn't be reductionist or reifying that either. And we shouldn't be making proletarians into religious icons, and so on. So there is even still more rupturing to be done.

The truth is important to the proletariat in two senses—or should be. One, it is important in the same way that beauty is important, or should be important. Yes, as opposed to the truth, different people do have different social viewpoints on what is beautiful. The truth doesn't have a social content in that sense. It just objectively exists. But knowing the truth (or approximating the truth) is important in the same way beauty is important (even while people's differing class viewpoints will lead them to have different conceptions, or notions, about what beauty is and what is and is not beautiful). And there is this process, as I was speaking to earlier—how truths enter into the class struggle in a very non-reductionist way.

Why do I say the truth is good for the proletariat? Because the more we know about the world, the better we are going to be able to transform it toward the objective of communism. We cannot torture the truth to fit into our narrow conceptions of what communism is and how to get there. But if we view it correctly, the more truth there is in the world, the better it is for the cause of communism. Even if the truth includes truths about bad things that communists do. That is the point about truths that make us cringe. Even the aspect of the truth that is the ugly side of what our project has brought forth, the errors that have been made and the ways in which we have sometimes made a mess of things (and actual horrors that have been created by people who have acted in the name of communism), even those truths, actual truths, not lies—those truths, strategically, if they are approached with the correct methodology, can be part of strengthening the struggle for communism. These negative aspects are definitely not the main thing about our project, they are *not* what has characterized the rule of the proletariat and socialist society in historical experience so far, they are *not* the main thing with regard to what real, as opposed to phony, communists have done; and we do have to answer the claim that this is the case and the slanders that are put forward to heap abuse on our whole project— those slanders too are a fundamental distortion of the truth. But to arrive at and fight for the correct synthesis in all this, which takes into account both the essence of things but also the contradictoriness and complexity of it all, you have to have the right outlook and methodology.

So I think that is worth thinking about and wrangling with. Is this right or wrong? The more I grapple with this, the more I firmly believe this. But let's talk about this. Let's really wrestle with this. This involves a big rupture. It is not what has been the convention for how communists conceive of and approach these things.

It is not just that we are not afraid of the truth. That is true. But the other side of this is that we have an approach of embracing and then synthesizing—not just taking experience and partial knowledge as it is but embracing it and synthesizing it in its fullest dimensions and to its richest depths.

HOW WE KNOW WHAT WE KNOW: DEVELOPMENTS IN THE MATERIAL WORLD, DEVELOPMENTS IN HUMAN KNOWLEDGE

Here is something from our practice that provides an important lesson ideologically—against religious tendencies and in favor of science. A comrade described a conversation with someone who is in the field of medicine, who said: "What I learned in medical school, they tell me now that a bunch of that's wrong, and twenty years from now what I believe to be true now, they'll say *that's* wrong. So how do you know if anything's true?"

Well, there is motion and development, and there are principal and secondary aspects to things. We are not religious people. If you find a flaw in something, does that necessarily invalidate the whole thing? In any field of science that I know of, people are working on solving problems and they come up with a lot of breakthroughs, but then there's something wrong with a particular aspect of it. Does that mean you throw the whole thing out and start over? No! You sort it out. People do this in the sciences even somewhat spontaneously, that is, without dialectical materialism, or without a systematic application of dialectical materialism. You sort out what's correct from what's incorrect and build on the former and discard the latter, and you keep doing it.

It isn't true that nobody can know anything. To take one important example, we know a lot more about diseases of various kinds than we did 100 years ago, even though some particular verdicts have been reversed and it does get confusing sometimes.

This is a good lesson for people concerning the dialectical motion of knowledge and the scientific method overall, and the materialist approach to these things as opposed to a religious approach.

"BUSHISM" AND COMMUNISM

What is the solid core with a lot of elasticity?[1] What *is* this synthesis? If anybody thinks it's liberalism, they are missing the whole point, to say the least.

It's not hard to be a liberal. It's not hard to have all elasticity—or at least to proclaim that as an ideal—that's the idealized vision of bourgeois democracy. In fact, you can't actually have all elasticity, but to articulate that as a line is very easy, and it's been a well trodden path. Lots of people have done it—some of them in the communist movement, most of them outside of it. What this bourgeois ideal translates into, in reality, is polarization in society between those with wealth and power and those without—it leads to perpetuating exploitation, oppression, and massive inequalities. That is the essential nature of bourgeois society, and that is the experience of living under the dictatorship of the bourgeoisie, including in the form of bourgeois democracy. (This is discussed at length in my book *Democracy: Can't We Do Better Than That*, and is spoken to in my more recent talk: *Dictatorship and Democracy, and the Socialist Transition to Communism*.)

It's very easy to have all solid core—or a one-sided emphasis on

---

1. Avakian discusses this concept in the talk *Dictatorship and Democracy, and the Socialist Transition to Communism* as follows: "[Y]ou have to have a solid core that firmly grasps and is committed to the strategic objectives and aims and process of the struggle for communism. If you let go of that you are just giving everything back to the capitalists in one form or another, with all the horrors that means. At the same time, if you don't allow for a lot of diversity and people running in all kinds of directions with things, then not only are people going to be building up tremendous resentment against you, but you are also not going to have the rich kind of process out of which the greatest truth and ability to transform reality will emerge." ("A World We Would Want to Live In," *Revolutionary Worker* #1257 [October 31, 2004].)

solid core—that's been the history of a lot of the communist movement, frankly, when it's gotten right down to it, and especially whenever anybody's been under pressure.

What is the essence of this, and what is difficult to handle correctly, is the *synthesis* of the two—solid core and elasticity. *That* is what I have been bringing forward and giving emphasis to—speaking to how you handle this moving dialectic of the synthesis of the two. And I also emphasize the words "the moving dialectic." That's what's hard, and that's what is new. That's the challenge and that's what is new in terms of how it applies to the party and in terms of how it applies to the dictatorship of the proletariat and socialist society. That is why, in a discussion on epistemology, I raised the metaphor of being drawn and quartered,[2] because it is very difficult to handle this correctly, to apply this principle of "solid core with a lot of elasticity" in the correct way in leading a party, a revolutionary struggle, and a new socialist society precisely in transition toward the goal of a communist world.

And the fact is, if there's not a solid core, you can forget about *any* of this: The whole sweep of history from here to where we're trying to go—to communism, worldwide—you can forget all of that, if there's no solid core.

I think we really have to understand what is being talked about here. People should understand, for example, that the question of democratic centralism in a communist party is being spoken to. Do people recognize that what's in the talk on the dictatorship of the proletariat[3] about solid core and elasticity is addressing problems with democratic centralism, including the "too much centralism" aspect? Do people realize I'm trying to grapple with the historic problems of having a party like this, that there are historic problems? It's like having an army during the struggle to get to communism: You can't do without it, but it's a big problem having it, especially when you are in power, but not only then.

To speak honestly, and bluntly, there is a lot of "Bushism" in the communist movement. There is a lot of what is quoted from an actual Bushite in that article by Ron Suskind:[4] "'We're an empire now,' an aide

---

2. See "Bob Avakian in a Discussion with Comrades on Epistemology: On Knowing and Changing the World," selection 5 in this volume.

3. This refers to the talk *Dictatorship and Democracy, and the Socialist Transition to Communism*, mentioned above.

4. Ron Suskind, "Without a Doubt," *The New York Times Magazine*, (October 17, 2004).

to the president told me, 'and when we act, we create our own reality. And while you're studying that reality—judiciously, as you will—we'll act again, creating other new realities.'" Right now the imperialists act like this, but some communists want to have the same outlook. This is something we have to completely, profoundly rupture with.

* * * * *

Why do some people think that the banner of communism is "tattered" if there have been shortcomings? That is a religious viewpoint. You pull one little thread and it all unravels—that's religion, religious absolutism. This is the point I keep hammering at about the Christian Fascists: If one thing in the Bible is wrong, then their whole case is sunk. That is because they are Christian Fascists. They are not communists. They are Christian Fascists who have to put their religious-based views forward as an absolute that can't have any fault in it. This is why I keep hammering at this point about these Christian Fascists. Some people might think I am obsessed with this and I am fanatical about this myself and I'm undialectical about it or idealist about it. But I have some strategic thinking about how the way you can get to the mass base of these Christian Fascists is by hammering at the foundation of it. The way you can win people away from it—or one of the keys to doing that, reality itself will also have an effect—is by hammering in the ideological sphere, hammering at this contradiction between the absolutism of it and the fact that there are some things in a literal interpretation of the Bible that are, to put it mildly, embarrassing even for fundamentalist Christians to try to uphold right at this particular juncture—although, if we don't hurry up, even that won't be true for very long. So I have some thinking that goes into this—about why the coherence of this is vulnerable to attack, ideologically—because these people are idealists, absolutists. They are not scientists. They can't accept a flaw.

But that's a "disease," ideologically speaking, that has also affected communists, including our party. But why should we be afraid of the truth, even truth about the shortcomings of our project and what has happened in socialist society?

I'm not afraid of what anybody learns in astrophysics. I'm not afraid of bourgeois democracy. I don't think somebody is going to prove that bourgeois democracy is better than the dictatorship of the proletariat, so I'm not afraid of bourgeois democracy—that is what I mean by that. But people are afraid, because they're not scientific—they're afraid that something is going to come along to show that really, after all, bourgeois democracy and capitalism is the best that we can possibly have. And then, with that outlook, you just cling to your own form of "Bushism": We're going to create a reality that blots out all the things that we don't like to think about. There's a path that takes you down. But that is completely opposed to what Marxism is, and should be, all about. And we should be Marxists—basing ourselves on the most critical, creative, profoundly, systematically and comprehensively scientific approach.

A SCIENTIFIC APPROACH TO MAOISM, A SCIENTIFIC APPROACH TO SCIENCE

There is a nationalist conception of Maoism, a "Third Worldist" conception of Maoism, and there is a corresponding understanding of, not just the political elements of Maoism and Marxism generally but also of the philosophical elements. For example, take the question of principal contradiction: what is the principal contradiction in the world, at any given time, and how can this be determined? Some people have picked up this formulation that came out of the 9th Congress of the Chinese Communist Party and out of *Long Live the Victory of People's War* (a document written by Lin Biao in the mid-1960s),[1] about how the principal contradiction in the world is between the oppressed nations (or the Third World) and imperialism. To be honest, I don't believe some people have done much thinking beyond that—their attitude is: "The Third World is where the 'storm centers' of the world revolution are, that's the principal contradiction, what's the discussion?" It has been 40 years since *Long Live the Victory of People's War* was written, and 35 years since the 9th Congress—and in its 10th Congress the Chinese Party didn't even repeat that formulation (on the principal con-

---

1. Lin Biao was a veteran of the Long March and the Chinese revolution overall, and during the first phases of the Cultural Revolution in China, in the mid and late 1960s, he was not only a leader of the Chinese Communist Party but was actually designated for a time as Mao's successor. But in 1971 he developed differences with Mao over important issues, apparently having to do not only with the continuation of the revolution in China itself but also with China's relations with the Soviet Union on the one hand and the U.S. on the other hand; these differences led Lin Biao into antagonistic opposition to Mao and the policies Mao was pursuing, and in the course of seeking to foment what amounted to a coup against Mao's leadership, Lin Biao ended up being killed himself.

tradiction in the world being between the oppressed nations and imperialism) as I recall. Instead, they talked about the major world contradictions being in flux at that time, or made some general statement of
that kind.

And there has been a tendency to become sort of "stuck" and to
try to "freeze" reality in accordance with how things were formulated
in Mao's pre-1949 writings—Mao's writings before the victory of the
new-democratic revolution in China, before power was seized throughout the country, in 1949, and the revolution entered into the socialist
stage. Along with this, uneven attention has been paid to the whole theoretical dimension of the Great Proletarian Cultural Revolution in
China and the struggle against capitalist restoration—the whole theoretical dimension of continuing the revolution under the dictatorship of
the proletariat—all the theoretical work that was done, including in the
last great battle against revisionism in China in the early 1970s,[2] theoretical work dealing with the questions of the relation between the base
and the superstructure in socialist society, formulations like "power
over the means and relations of production is concentrated in the
power of political leadership." These are important theoretical conceptions to be engaging.

* * * * *

We have to have a scientific approach to science. There are all
kinds of funny tendencies among communists—for example, reducing
our ideology of Marxism-Leninism-Maoism to political strategy, with
maybe some political economy thrown in.

The whole idea of "embraces but does not replace"—there have
been problems with people not understanding the second aspect of that
in particular. That is a lot of what I have been speaking to, especially in
the talk on the dictatorship of the proletariat: the emphasis on the "does
not replace" aspect.[3] But there has also been a narrowness reflected in

---

2. The "last great battle" refers to the struggle, led by Mao until his death in
1976, to beat back the attempts of the revisionists (phony communists) in China,
with Deng Xiaoping as their most notorious leader, to overthrow socialism and
restore capitalism.

3. "Embraces but does not replace" refers to a principle formulated by Mao
Tsetung that Marxism embraces but does not replace the various spheres of science
and art, and other realms of human thought and endeavor. This concept has been
further developed and applied by Bob Avakian. See, for example, his discussion of
this in *Dictatorship and Democracy, and the Socialist Transition to Communism* (available online at revcom.us) and "Marxism 'Embraces But Does Not Replace,'" which
appears in this volume.

people not understanding the *first* part of this—that Marxism does embrace all these different spheres. Marxism is an outlook and methodology for engaging *all of reality*.

The point of "does not replace" is that you have to go into the particularity of contradiction. You have to go into the particulars of any sphere of human knowledge and endeavor. I think this has been seen in a very instrumentalist way, not only in the sense of "truth as an organizing principle,"[4] but in another sense—seeing Marxism-Leninism-Maoism itself as a narrow instrument: as an instrument for making a new-democratic revolution; or an instrument for developing a military strategy; and so on.

Theory is a guide to practice—that is another thing that has been vulgarized. The point that theory originates in practice and finds its ultimate verification in practice has been vulgarized. Even the sources of Marxism have been vulgarized. Marxism is not just a summation of the class struggle or of revolution. Marx and Engels did not develop Marxism by just summing up the class struggle. There was much broader, more sweeping experience of human society, in many different spheres and dimensions, that was being encompassed in the development of Marxism.

I was really struck, when I went back and re-read *Anti-Duhring* in the last year or so: it covers all kinds of things. I was very struck by the whole orientation at the end of it. It is exactly a scientific one: of course a lot of these things that are understood to be true now will be superseded and more will be learned. The whole orientation is so different than what is unfortunately all too common among communists these days—there has been (if you'll pardon a perhaps unfortunate phrase) a sort of "circling of the wagons" around this ideology, besides tendencies

---

4. "Truth as an organizing principle" is a concept that Lenin criticized and dissected in his major philosophical work *Materialism and Empirio-Criticism*. "Truth as an organizing principle" refers to an approach where, instead of investigating and coming to know reality as it actually is, and seeking to transform it on that basis, you try to impose a vision of reality which appears to be useful to your purposes, and then try to "organize"—or torture—reality to make it fit your preconceived, "useful" notion of it. In political movements—including, unfortunately, within the communist movement at times—this kind of conception and approach has found expression in the notion of "political truths" (or "politically useful truths") which are in fact not truths at all but distortions of reality; and such "truths," and even more fundamentally the outlook and methodology that leads to the distortion of reality in this way, constitute obstacles to actually understanding reality and really, radically transforming it.

to turn it into a religion. This is reflected in the notion that "we shouldn't make public criticism." [This refers to comments by some comrades in the international movement, in response to the publication of some talks and writings by Bob Avakian which raised criticism of Lenin, particularly around the conception of dictatorship—specifically Lenin's definition of dictatorship as rule unrestricted by laws.] You wouldn't take that kind of approach in any other field of science—no scientists in any other field would argue that those who have made important breakthroughs should not be publicly criticized!

Even the point from Marx's *Theses on Feuerbach*—that the purpose, after all, is to change the world and the philosophers have only sought to understand it—this can be and has been vulgarized. Of course, the purpose is to change things. In any sphere of science the purpose is ultimately to change the world. But not in a narrow way, not always in an immediate sense, not in a utilitarian sense.

We have come up within that same tradition. With Mao, I think, especially if you read his more unofficial writings and talks, there is a lot of stuff in there that goes against that grain of instrumentalism. In the Soviet Union, they had all kinds of people doing science. But there was this problem—not only the Lysenko fiasco,[5] but someone was

---

5. Avakian has characterized the situation with Lysenko as follows: "Lysenko was an agronomist, a botanist, who claimed to have brought forward new strains of wheat that would make production leap ahead in agriculture. And this was a real problem in the Soviet Union, that agriculture was seriously lagging industry. And, of course, if that gap continues to widen it throws the whole economy out of whack and basically unhinges your attempts to build a socialist economy. So this was a very severe problem they were facing, particularly in the early and mid 1930s. And Lysenko basically brought forward a theory which contradicted basic principles of evolution and fell into the whole idea of the inheritability of acquired characteristics and so on, which is not scientifically correct. But pragmatically it seemed like a way to solve the agricultural problems, so Stalin and others threw a lot of weight behind Lysenko. And this did a lot of damage. Not only in the short run and in a more narrow sense—it didn't lead to the results that they were hoping for—but it also did a lot of damage in the broader sense in terms of how people were being trained to think, and how they were being trained to handle the relationship between theory and practice, and reality and understanding and transforming reality. There's a way in which this has had long-term negative consequences. First of all, it did in the Soviet Union. And it did in the international communist movement, because it trained people to think in a certain erroneous way.

"Now, this situation was very complicated, because many of the people who were the experts and authorities in the field of biology, botany, and so on in the Soviet Union were carried forward from the old society. And many of them were

telling me that they set out to prove that Einstein was wrong because Einstein was not a dialectical materialist. And it turns out that Einstein was wrong about some things, but not because he wasn't [*laughter*]...yes, it is related to his not being a dialectical materialist, but not in that one-to-one kind of way.

This goes back to an earlier point about how I don't agree with this thing from *Anti-Duhring* about philosophy—that Marxism basically put an end to philosophy, as such.[6] But, in a certain sense, Engels can be forgiven for saying that Marxism put an end to philosophy as such (and that all that remained was dialectics and formal logic) because when something gets newly discovered, you don't yet have the historical perspective to fully put it all in the correct context. At one and the same time you have Engels saying that Marxism has put an end to philosophy, as such; and, on the other hand, you see this "open-endedness" at the end of *Anti-Duhring*. It is kind of a contradiction. But you don't necessarily see things in their full context when they are first coming into being. That is what I mean by saying Engels can be forgiven in a certain sense. But to keep clinging to that kind of stuff—that's no good.

Are we going to have a scientific approach to our science or not? This doesn't mean we are retreating into "contemplative philosophy"— just thinking about, or contemplating, things for its own sake, in the sense of not trying to change the world. What I have tried to bring forward is a different way of approaching understanding and changing the world, including that I took the Mao formulation about "embraces but does not replace" and developed it more in terms of the whole dialectical process between Marxism and other schools of thought. What I am arguing for, in regard to "embraces but does not replace," is a very complex thing. It is a very dynamic thing. It is grounded in the understanding and orientation that, ultimately and in a fundamental sense, we can and should embrace everything. Marxism is a way of engaging all of reality, not just some parts of it.

---

political and ideological reactionaries. So here you see the contradiction is very acutely posed. Lysenko was trying to make a breakthrough to advance the socialist cause, and being opposed by authorities, many of whom—not all, but many of whom—were political and ideological reactionaries. But it just so happened that they were more correct than him about the basic point at issue. Yet political expediency dictated what was done there, and the people who were critical were actually suppressed." (See "The Struggle in the Realm of Ideas," in this volume.)

6. See "Marxism Is a Science, It Is Not 'The End of Philosophy,'" in this volume.

Communism and Different Schools of Thought

And this does pose an interesting philosophical question about what happens when you get to communism. What I believe is that at that point schools of thought will pose themselves differently. And I am trying to develop the understanding that it is actually *good* to have a clash of schools of thought. At this stage it is even good to have the clash between Marxist and non-Marxist schools of thought. Not because Marxism is not capable of ultimately embracing everything, but because you don't want to turn it into a "closed system." And while all Marxists should learn to think as creatively and critically as anybody— or more so—it is also good, for this whole period, to have the dynamic between that and people who are not Marxists, or at least not consistently Marxists.

I suppose you could say that this represents a "united front led by the proletariat in the ideological sphere," in a certain sense. Even though there is only one ideology that, as communists, we can base ourselves on—only one ideology that, correctly understood and applied, is thoroughly in line with material reality and its motion and development—it is also true that, because of the nature of knowledge and of human beings, and the limitations of that...let me see if I can understand this myself...because of the limitations on the knowledge of human beings, not only individually but even collectively, because of the way human beings acquire knowledge and the relation between theory and practice, there is a certain role... Here is a funny way to look at it—you know the thing about how Marxism has to be brought "from the outside"?—from outside the realm of people's direct experience— well, I am also arguing that there is, at least at this stage of history, a certain role for things to be brought *from outside Marxism*, which Marxism then integrates to a deeper level than the non-Marxist people who bring them forward can ever do. The Marxists should synthesize these things into a deeper understanding of reality. I'm just sort of being "trippy" here, but my point is that there is some way that, whatever the communists are able to encompass—I'm talking about philosophically and methodologically—whatever they are able to encompass at a given time, there are going be others, who objectively are not going to be communists, who are going to be poking their sticks at the same problems. Not that we need Marxism and non-Marxism in *our* ideology. That is not the point—to be clear. But Marxism itself can get enriched by being able, *through the application of Marxism*, to integrate those things that are done by non-Marxists.

We can't do everything. Marxists can't do everything that is involved in the investigation of reality at any given time. I think that probably when you get to communism, then there will be different schools of thought, but that will be in a whole different framework. And they probably won't call it "communism" then—but they'll have different schools of thought once they get very far into communism. I have frequently used this as an example: When you're sick—you have a cold or the flu—and then you get well, you don't remember exactly the moment you got well. You just all of sudden look back and think, "I don't feel sick any more." Well, it probably will be the same thing in getting to communism. [laughter] My point is that probably communism, "from the other side," won't look the way we envision it now, not only in the sense that we can't anticipate certain things but also in the sense that when they get to "the other side" of it, they'll see the contradictions in it differently than how we can foresee this now. So, at a certain point, they'll say, "All that talk about communism isn't relevant any more because now we are into a whole different set of contradictions that we're dealing with." Not that the dialectical materialist viewpoint and method will no longer still apply. That is not my point. They will just be approaching things differently and see the contradictions differently.

The point of all this is that the methodology we need is opposed to a rigid, schematic, "let me see if I can get the formula" approach. As a comrade was just saying, "the caravan moves on." Life continues to evolve, reality continues to unfold. It is a little bit like Engels' point about motion—motion being itself a contradiction. Something is in one place and not in one place at one and the same time. This is all moving stuff. It is a little bit like the theory of relativity. Having moved on, you don't see the reality the same way as you saw it when you were "within" it, at a point in the past. We saw it a certain way then, and we don't see it the same way when more reality unfolds. So understanding it—understanding something from the past—has something to do with understanding new things too—understanding the past according to what you have learned from those new things, or what you have to learn. That's why you can't just stop the motion of things and say "freeze, extract a part, let's study it" all unto itself. You *can* do that *relatively*, but you can't really, completely do it that way. You can say, "let's take a month and study the Great Proletarian Cultural Revolution," but you're not going to see it the same way as you did in the past. It has already divided into two again. The understanding of that Great Proletarian Cultural Revolution has already divided into two again, because matter is moving on. You cannot approach it now the way you approached it then—you can't see it the same way now as you saw it then. You are going to see it differently in one way or another.

This is not to argue that "everything is relative," and that it is impossible to really arrive at an understanding of objective truth. No, things can be known, and some things can be determined with absolute certainty—relatively. In other words, as Lenin emphasized in his philosophical writings, there is an element of the relative in the absolute (and vice versa), but that is different than saying there is *only* relative and not absolute knowledge of things—and that difference, as Lenin pointed out, represents a fundamental dividing line between Marxists and relativists, who deny any possibility, or any aspect, of absolute truth, and therefore ultimately, and at least objectively, deny the possibility of knowing anything with any degree of certainty.

I really believe that it is extremely important to continue grappling with basic questions of methodology. Now, sometimes you cannot grasp the correct methodology because you are approaching things with a different methodology! That is a real, and sometimes acute, contradiction. But that is the role of struggle in the realm of ideology and methodology. As I pointed out to Bill Martin, for a long time that was our problem with the question of homosexuality and our party's incorrect, negative view on this.[7] We couldn't get the point because our methodology didn't allow us to get it. But then we kept working on things and being struggled with in various ways, and looking at different aspects of reality—and eventually this can cause you to begin to see this particular thing differently too.

The Relation of Practice and Theory—Correctly Understood

There was some tendency epistemologically toward empiricism in Mao, too. For example, his essential reply to people about how to make revolution in other countries: "don't copy" [what they did in China]. That is not sufficient. That is not literally all he said, of course, but that was pretty much the essential message: "Don't copy, you have to find your own path." There was an epistemological element to that which

---

7. See Bob Avakian and Bill Martin, *Marxism and the Call of the Future: Conversations on Ethics, History, and Politics* (Chicago: Open Court, 2005), chapter 21; and *On the Position on Homosexuality in the Draft Programme* (Chicago: RCP Publications, 2001).

wasn't right. Yes, of course, you can't make revolution anywhere by trying to repeat the Chinese revolution literally. But there is something epistemologically wrong about just saying that and not further engaging what people are grappling with in trying to make revolution in their countries, frankly. Why shouldn't the Chinese party wrangle with people about the problems of the revolution in their countries? You could always have reminded them of what Mao said about Stalin if they got too heavy-handed. [This refers to Mao's statement that in China they made revolution by acting contrary to Stalin's will.]

There is an epistemological element involved in this, which ties in with the question of the relation of the revolution in a particular country to the world struggle and specifically the tendency to raise up the situation and the struggle in a particular country as an arena unto itself. Mao made statements that are contrary to that: As for the imperialist countries, they are among us and we are among them. In saying this, Mao was referring to the fact that in the socialist countries there are counter-revolutionaries who support imperialism, while in the imperialist countries there are people whose fundamental interests lie with revolution. He wasn't all one-sided. But there was a tendency there toward nationalism and related epistemology.

The reason for raising this is that it does exist in our movement—and it ties in with the question of how to correctly understand the relation of theory and practice. Tied in with nationalism and "Third Worldism," there is a form of empiricism which narrowly treats theory and its relation to practice. Fundamentally, this involves a misrepresentation of what science is and how science works—it does not represent the correct understanding of the relation of theory to practice. In today's world especially, anybody can study the practice of just about anything in the world and can draw theoretical abstractions out of that practice, as well as other things. Anybody can do that. People in any part of the world can make analyses—and do, for that matter—about the U.S. They don't have to reside in the U.S. or be engaged in the practice of trying to change the U.S. to be able to draw correct theoretical abstractions of sometimes great significance, or possibly great significance, about the U.S. This is because of the way the world is and the way knowledge is in relation to that.

The correct orientation toward and the correct understanding of practice and its relation to theoretical abstractions is this: We should all try to develop revolutionary theory *because the world needs it*, the world revolutionary struggle *needs* it. Try to fulfill that great need, wherever you are. And wherever you are, irrespective of the level of revolutionary struggle there at a given time, if you do develop the most advanced theory, everyone will—or everyone should—gladly embrace it, take it up and apply it. But that is not because there is a one-to-one relationship between that theory and whatever the level of your struggle is at a given time. That is not the correct understanding of the criterion of truth.

The criterion of truth is whether something corresponds to reality or not. That does ultimately reside in practice, but not in a narrow, empiricist sense. This is where it gets complicated. I think this methodological question is the most important thing. Not that it is all we have to struggle over, but one of the problems that has been bugging me for years and years is that in a lot of things I have done, I have pointed to some decisive contradictions, and I keep trying to help come up with resolutions to them, but as far as I have gotten in a lot of spheres is pointing to these contradictions—for example, all the changes going on in the world, the underlying material changes and the demographic effects, and then the ideological, cultural, and social effects of that, the phenomena associated with that in the ideological, cultural, and social sphere. There is massive upheaval of the peasantry throughout the Third World. All I've been able to do at this point is pose questions that we need to wrestle with about what that means in terms of strategy and tactics of the revolutionary struggle. I have some thoughts about that. But one of the problems—and here's a real irony—is that there is a definite need for people who are running up against this more directly and fully in practice to also be part of wrangling with this. There is a lot to be learned about this. Not that we should reduce it to direct experience, or that such people are the only ones who have anything to say about this—or that what they have to say about it *ipso facto* (merely by the fact that they are saying it) makes it closer to the truth. But this is something for the whole international movement to take up. This cannot be solved by people in one country, and certainly not by any one person.

I feel very strongly that the question of methodology is of decisive importance. It is a matter of struggle—even among communists!!—to even get communism recognized as a science, instead of essentially a religion and "an organizing principle." Then there is the question—not that this should be done in stages, first one and then the other, but there is also the question—of having a scientific approach to the science. These are all bound up together, and this has a lot of manifestations. For example, once again, whether we dare to critically examine our own history—the way scientists do. And this is the orientation that is in *The Declaration of the RIM*,[8] after all—at least in the sense that it talks about how you have to correctly handle the dialectic between upholding and creatively developing communist theory and principles. At least the spirit is in there that you ought to examine these things and be able to divide one into two. When Marx and Engels examined the experience of the Paris Commune, they made a *critical summation* of that experience. What would we think if someone were to say that they should not have critically summed up the Commune, because it was a heroic experience? That is alien to what we should be all about, in terms of orientation and methodology.

We have to recognize the importance of all this—this whole question of method and approach to the science itself as well as to particular problems—and the importance of the unity between grasping and applying Marxism as a way to engage all of reality, on the one hand, and its particular application to the problems of making revolution, on the other hand. I think that is also a very important unity of opposites: the unity of opposites between grasping and applying Marxism as a way of engaging *all of reality*—every sphere of reality—in accordance with the "embraces but does not replace" understanding, or principle, on the one hand; and, on the other hand, applying Marxism to the actual problems of transforming the world in the political sphere—making revolution. There is a unity of opposites there. And this is related to the point that if you don't have a poetic spirit, it is a real problem. (This refers to the part of my talk from fifteen years ago, "The End of a Stage—The Beginning of a New Stage,"[9] where I cite Mao's statements that "Whenever the mind becomes rigid, it is very dangerous" and "If you are too realistic, you can't write poetry," and then I comment: "And I would add, in keeping with the thrust of what Mao is saying here, that if you don't have a poetic spirit— or at least a poetic side—it is very dangerous for you to lead a Marxist movement or be the leader of a socialist state.") If you don't have the kind of all-engaging approach to reality I've been talking about, you're not going to do well with revolution, and the kind of revolution you are going to try to make is not going to be very good.

---

8. *The Declaration of the Revolutionary Internationalist Movement* was adopted by the delegates and observers at the Second International Conference of Marxist-Leninist Parties and Organisations which formed the Revolutionary Internationalist Movement (RIM) in 1984.

9. Avakian, "The End of a Stage—The Beginning of a New Stage" (late 1989), in *Revolution* No. 60 (Fall 1990).

SOLID CORE WITH A LOT OF ELASTICITY: EPISTEMOLOGY AND APPLICATION

Getting back to the solid core with a lot of elasticity—and along with that a point that is also in the DOP talk ("Dictatorship and Democracy, and the Socialist Transition to Communism")[1] on the importance of distinguishing between those times and circumstances when you can and need to draw clear and firm conclusions and insist on things, and those times and circumstances when you cannot and/or should not do that, when it would do more harm than good to do it, because there is not the need or the basis to do it—as I've emphasized, this whole principle of solid core with a lot of elasticity, and this principle of drawing this distinction between these different times and circumstances, applies not only to the dictatorship of the proletariat but applies all the way through the struggle from here to communism—and applies within the party as well. I've read reports where comrades were saying, "That doesn't apply within the party, the party *is* the solid core." No. Wrong.

This relates to the principle Mao articulated about how what's universal in one context is particular in another, and that there is a dialectical relation between universal and particular. What is universal in one context is particular in another (and vice versa) because the range of things is vast and because of the interconnectedness of things, Mao said. What is a "solid core" in one context is "elasticity" in another (and vice versa). There is no such thing as all solid core with no elasticity, or all elasticity with no solid core. Even on the leading levels of a

---

1. Bob Avakian, *Dictatorship and Democracy, and the Socialist Transition to Communism* (excerpted in the *Revolutionary Worker* from August through December 2004 and available online at revcom.us).

party there needs to be solid core and elasticity. The solid core is real but relative, elasticity is relative too and dependant on the solid core. But the solid core itself is relative, it has room in it for things to move around, otherwise everything will grind to a halt and you won't have any solid core, or elasticity. Or you'll have the wrong kind of solid core and the wrong kind of elasticity coexisting—you'll have some kind of combination of dogmatic rigidity with, at the same time, relativism and eclectics and bourgeois liberalism. So this applies in the party and on every level of the party. Fundamentally, it is a way of seeing and of approaching reality.

And it is difficult. Some people have said that only certain people can grasp and apply this. That is not the point, it is for everyone to grasp and apply this kind of approach and method. Yes, it is hard, it is much harder than proceeding in a bureaucratic straight line march—which doesn't lead you where you need to go. That may feel more safe and comfortable in a certain framework, until you look around and see the larger world that is impinging on you. Yes, this is hard but it is also exhilarating. I was having a discussion with another comrade about this question and how this has arisen in relation to a young comrade who has been a student of astrophysics. It revolves around the beginning of the DOP talk: can you be an astrophysicist and be in the party? My orientation is: well, why not? I'm not afraid of anything that they might discover in the sphere of astrophysics. I'm not afraid of anything about reality that anybody might discover. That's not personal braggadocio; it's a matter of orientation I'm stressing. Yes, some of it will be difficult and yes, there are truths that make us cringe. But why should we be afraid of anything about reality that's really true? If god existed then we wouldn't need to be communists! Okay, then we wouldn't have to worry so much. God does *not* exist, so we need to be communists. We have to keep digging into reality, we have to encourage people to dig into reality.

I was interested in reading the physicist Brian Greene's book *The Fabric of the Cosmos* where (and this is very rare) he actually mentions Lenin's philosophical work *Materialism and Empirio-Criticism*—and does so without the seemingly obligatory dumping on it or on Lenin! I was really struck by that. He just mentions it in passing, but not negatively. A lot of people out there are engaging with a lot of reality with varying methods, and we should, yes, be struggling with them, we should be engaging them, but in a good way. Yes, astrophysicists should be out among the masses and learning from the masses, and they should go talk to the masses about astrophysics. We should play a role in helping them do that, because it is not so easy for them to do that— that is actually part of why you need a vanguard. And, yes, they should learn from the masses. Yes, comrades in these fields should sell our party's newspaper and distribute other party literature, and so on. But they also need to do their work in their fields and engage reality because we will all, including the vanguard, be much better off for it, if we work with them correctly, with the correct orientation.

MADISON, JEFFERSON, AND STALIN...
AND COMMUNISM AS A SCIENCE

There is a part in the *Memoir*[1]: Madison, Jefferson, and Stalin. I believe that is an apt analogy in both senses: in the sense that, if the bourgeoisie can uphold Madison and Jefferson, we can uphold Stalin, but also the other side of the analogy, referring to Stalin's very serious shortcomings from the standpoint of *our* revolution and our objectives. This is what we're doing—that's the analogy—we're upholding *our* Madisons and Jeffersons (and Madison and Jefferson were slave owners).

I read some documents by some communists in another part of the world, where they referred to "the great Stalin." That's just wrong. I believe we can uphold Stalin with historical perspective, and we should understand the historical context for that—but that's what we're doing. And to go around touting "the great Stalin" right now—I don't think that will lead to a world where people, including myself, would want to live.

You may achieve some significant things, but you're not going to get anywhere near communism with that line. On the other hand, as I have also emphasized many times, it is not a matter of throwing out the baby with the bath water: To throw out the historical experience of socialist society, including in the Soviet Union, because of serious errors made under Stalin, would be wrong—it would represent a wrong analysis of that historical experience, of reality. No, the correct understanding is captured in: Madison, Jefferson, and Stalin, as I have spoken to it.

---

1. *From Ike to Mao and Beyond: My Journey from Mainstream America to Revolutionary Communist, a Memoir by Bob Avakian* (Chicago: Insight Press, 2005), pp. 433-35.

And there were real shortcomings to Mao too. Recognizing that is also part of being an historical materialist. When I did an interview fairly recently with Michael Slate for his radio show[2], we talked about China and the Cultural Revolution and some of the things like the slogan "make the past serve the present and foreign things serve China." I said that's no good, especially the "foreign things serve China" is no good, it's not proletarian internationalism. There was no small amount of nationalism with Mao, including in the form of "Third Worldism" (onesidedly proceeding from the fact that, since World War 2, the Third World has been the main arena of revolutionary struggle against imperialism, tending to make an absolute out of that, as though all prospect of revolution in the imperialist countries themselves had essentially been eliminated, or removed to only the very distant future, after revolution had succeeded in vast parts of the Third World; and, along with that, a tendency to blur class distinctions within Third World countries, as well as within the imperialist countries).

So these things are contradictory. As materialists it shouldn't surprise us that Mao had shortcomings. I'm not for taking his name down. I'm not for no longer saying Marxism-Leninism-Maoism. I'm not for doing this with Mao or with Lenin or Marx. But they all had shortcomings. That was the point of my talk *Conquer the World*[3]: Not to say, "Ohhh, look how great *we* are, we can criticize everybody's shortcomings," but to recognize that this is a science. People are engaged in trying to change the world with imperialists pointing guns at their heads, and they make mistakes for that reason and because of shortcomings in outlook and methodology.

But there has been a definite tendency in the communist movement to say that Marxism is not a science, it's an ideology. Translation: religion. An ideology that is not a science is a religion (or tantamount to a religion). I didn't know that Engels wrote a book called Socialism: Utopian and *Ideological* (rather than the real title: *Socialism: Utopian and Scientific*). [laughter] Or that Marx and Engels called it "*ideological* socialism" (instead of "scientific socialism," which is how they often referred to communist ideology). This is a *science*. Scientists make mistakes. And even the ones who make great contributions run up against

---

2. Michael Slate hosts the show "Beneath the Surface" on KPFK Radio and is a writer for *Revolution* newspaper (formerly known as the *Revolutionary Worker*).

3. Bob Avakian, *Conquer the World? The International Proletariat Must and Will* (*Revolution,* No. 50, December 1981).

their limitations, and people have to recast what they did and go forward again. You know, Einstein is a symbol of genius even in a bourgeois sense. He completely recast physics. But then Einstein ran into his limitations and turned into his opposite in some ways. Certain things he couldn't confront, and he kept doing bad science to try to get things to conform to his prejudices. That was the context for his statement that "God doesn't play dice with the universe," because he was trying to put more order in the universe on a level where you couldn't make it fit. So he made tremendous breakthroughs, but then he degenerated into some bad science, from what I understand at least. So what, should we throw out Einstein? No. But this is what happens. You have human beings who have limitations—even the ones who take up Marxism, which is the most systematic and comprehensive scientific outlook and method there is, *if* it is correctly grasped and applied—but even people who advance Marxism have limitations and they make mistakes. The people who come along contemporaneously with them should struggle with them. The people who come along behind them and are trying to go further should have a scientific attitude toward them and toward science.

It's not just that some people who consider themselves communists "don't get" this—some people *don't want* this. Some people are afraid of this. They resist it, they reject it. And, yes, some people hate it. Someone associated with the communist movement in another country said about *CTW*: "You are just saying our whole thing is a tattered banner." Why? Because they do want it to be a religion. But it's not. And it's not a tattered banner. What I am arguing for is taking up and applying communist ideology as a science, making a scientific summation of real world experience and a concentration—yes, as theoretical abstractions—of that experience and a whole broader human experience. That is what it means to understand communist ideology not as a religion but as a science—correctly understood and applied, it is the most thoroughly consistent, systematic, and comprehensive scientific outlook and methodology.

THE "GODLIKE POSITION OF THE PROLETARIAT," THE SWEEP OF HISTORY

I recognize that what I've been struggling to bring forward, in the sphere of epistemology (theory of knowledge), and how this relates to our whole approach to revolution and getting to communism—this goes up against all the safe and sure ways that actually lead to nowhere and lead to getting worse than nowhere, lead to getting smashed ultimately and maybe not that ultimately these days. This does have to do with what I've been emphasizing, with the formulation (originally, if I recall correctly, I brought this formulation forward in a talk entitled *Strategic Questions*[1]): "the godlike position of the proletariat." Recently I made some further comments about this in a discussion on epistemology.[2] And in *Phony Communism is Dead...Long Live **Real** Communism!*[3] there is a footnote where I commented on how Stalin made some

---

1. The section of *Strategic Questions*, another talk given by Bob Avakian, that discusses the "godlike position of the proletariat" has not been published. The concept is discussed in "Fighting Not Just for Revenge But To Emancipate All Humanity" from *Great Objectives and Grand Strategy* in *RW* #1140 (February 24, 2002) and "Holding Firmly to Basic Principles—But Not Being Bound by Convention or Superstition" from *Grasp Revolution, Promote Production: Questions of Outlook and Method, Some Points on the New Situation* in *RW* #1186 (February 9, 2003) available online at revcom.us. Excerpts from *Strategic Questions* appeared in *Revolutionary Worker* #881 and #884-893 (November 1996 through February 1997), and in *RW* #1176-78 (November 24 through December 8, 2002). They are available online at revcom.us.

2. "Bob Avakian in a Discussion with Comrades on Epistemology: On Knowing and Changing the World," in this volume.

3. Avakian, *Phony Communism Is Dead...Long Live Real Communism!*, 2nd edition (Chicago: RCP Publications, 2004), p. 123.

observations—basically good observations by Stalin in this case—about how Engels situated capitalism in its overall historical framework, and how only by doing so is it really possible to fully grasp the essential character and the historically limited role of capitalism. It's the same point of Marx to Weydemeyer. To paraphrase, Marx said: No credit is due to me for discovering the existence of classes, or the anatomy of classes, or the struggle between the classes; and then he goes on to talk about what it is that he did that *was* new—how he put the emergence of classes and the struggle between classes in the whole historical sweep of the different phases of the development of production and the class struggle leading to the dictatorship of the proletariat and the dictatorship of the proletariat in turn leading to a classless society (and no dictatorship).[4]

The "godlike position of the proletariat" has to do with all that sweep of history captured by Marx in that letter to Weydemeyer. Or what Stalin said about Engels: Again, that is the point of the footnote in *Phony/Real*—if you don't see capitalism in its historical context, then you can't see beyond it. The revisionists, the economists, the narrow reformists, don't see that, all they see is the most narrow construct of the workers and the bosses (or the masses and their oppressors, in more immediate and narrow terms). That's the Menshevism that has had a significant influence in the communist movement over a whole period of time, and our party has certainly not been free of this.

Mao said that when Chou En-Lai was in the Soviet Union in the 1950s, he told Chou En-lai to tell the Soviets: What's the big deal about what you've done? All you've done is produce so many million tons of steel and so many million tons of grain. What's the big deal? Well, in that same spirit I say: What is the big deal about the proletariat? There *is* a big deal about the proletariat, but only understood in the correct sense. To make a big deal out of the proletariat in an incorrect sense is the essence of economism. I have been re-reading the Sebastian Haffner book about the attempt at revolution in Germany after World War 1, *Failure of a Revolution*.[5] In reading this now, I have been thinking about the criticism raised against Lenin over the fact that, after they seized power, the character of the Soviets, the workers' councils, changed—

---

4. "Marx to Joseph Weydemeyer, March 5, 1852," in Marx and Engels, *Selected Letters* (Peking: Foreign Languages Press), p. 18.

5. Sebastian Haffner, *Failure of a Revolution: Germany 1918-1919* (Chicago: Banner Press, 1986).

how they were in effect subordinated to other structures of the state—and I was saying to myself: "You can't run a society with workers' councils. You can't have a socialist state, the dictatorship of the proletariat, made up of workers' councils, it's more complex than that." The proletariat, as I said in that discussion on epistemology, is a class that has a certain historical role. I used this analogy: You are sitting there on a mountain, metaphorically speaking, and you look at the sweep of history and a certain class comes forward at a certain time and, as a class, it has both the necessity and the ability and potential to take society to a whole different place. *That* is the way in which the proletariat is important—and not in any other way.

* * * * *

I'm reading a book by Tom Hayden about gangs, *Street Wars, Gangs and the Future of Violence.* He makes the estimate that, over a couple of decades, I don't remember the exact figure but something like 25,000 people have been killed in these gang wars in the U.S. How are we going to call on these youth among the masses, and masses more broadly—the families and friends, and so on, where everybody knows somebody who has been killed—how are we going to call on them to be the emancipators of humanity and to rise above this stuff, if we communists can't rise above even more petty things? Look at what the system is doing to people every day. And people in the more privileged strata—how they are insulting the masses every day. Yes, that stuff is real, people getting on the elevator with basic masses and clutching their purses, and basic masses going into the store and getting followed around or looked down upon by the people who work in the store who are maybe one notch above them, if that, economically or whatever. These things are real and they hurt. But what is the correct orientation and methodology for dealing with this?—that is the question.

When I gave the talk on *Elections, Democracy and Dictatorship, Revolution and Resistance* in one area, there was a question-and-answer period afterward. A professor (I refer to this in the epistemology discussion) raised a very good question. He said, "Look, I like a lot of the stuff that you are saying, but here's a challenge to you: How would you actually do better than what was done in the Soviet Union in the '20s and '30s or in China during the Cultural Revolution?" I was stressing that we have to do better the next time around in handling these contradictions, not suppressing people for dissenting and so on. That was a very tough question he raised [*laughter*], and I did my best with it under the circumstances. I am still thinking about it and still wrestling with it, and we all should be. But one of the things I brought out there is this: "You can look around this room and see masses who have been mistreated by others—not necessarily by other people here personally, but by the types of other people who are also sitting in this room. How are we going to deal with that, how are we going to lead?" And then I made the point: I don't believe in tailing people just because they have been oppressed. That is not what we are here for, and that is not what the masses need us to do. I emphasized that people need to be led to be the emancipators of humanity. They need to be led with a lofty outlook and line and to raise their sights way above revenge.

Yes, there should be an accounting of real crimes that have been committed—real crimes, committed by the ruling class, and all the horrors that have been perpetrated by this system, there has to be an accounting of that. And there are contradictions among the people that we are going to have to resolve that are very acute. These are not minor contradictions. But they have to be dealt with in a very different way, a qualitatively different way, than contradictions, antagonistic contradictions, between the people and the actual enemy—that is a very correct and important point that Mao made. And if we don't raise people's sights to being the emancipators of humanity, then we don't have a chance to sort out and handle all this correctly.

This is what masses of people should aspire to be: emancipators of humanity. There are many inspiring examples throughout the history of the struggle of our class and our cause where people have risen to this, but we can't lead them if we don't raise this standard, and frankly we can't ask anything less of them than this. And if you are going to demand it of the masses who have suffered terrible wrongs, then certainly we have to demand it of their vanguard—and this applies in everything we do, including what our basic methodology is.

METHODS AND PRINCIPLES

I have been thinking about this question of method: how people are trained to think. Take the experience of the Black Panther Party: sometimes we don't think about this epistemologically, but a whole bunch of people were trained to think in instrumentalist terms,[1] besides other things. "Power is the ability to define phenomena and cause them to act in the desired manner"—that was a major formulation put forward by Huey Newton and popularized by the Panthers. Well, in terms of epistemology (theory of knowledge and the relation of knowledge to reality and to changing reality), that is not really different than the "Bushite" statement (cited by Ron Suskind in that *New York Times Magazine* article[2]) that "we are an empire and we are creating our own reality and you can judiciously study it." Of course, Huey Newton's formulation was in the service of very different, radically different, political ends; but epistemologically it is not essentially different. If I recall correctly, I spoke to that in *A Horrible End, Or An End to the Horror?*[3] You should not underestimate the importance of world outlook, including methodology and epistemology in particular.

The masses are being trained ideologically one way or another. The church trains them in a certain way of thinking—or not thinking. This "not thinking" is actually a way of thinking—we're just saying

---

1. "Instrumentalist" or "instrumentalism" refers to an approach where you seek to make reality an "instrument" of your purposes and objectives, rather than investigating and coming to know reality as it actually is, through objective scientific methods, and seeking to change it on *that* basis.

2. Ron Suskind, "Without a Doubt," *The New York Times Magazine* (October 17, 2004).

3. Bob Avakian, *A Horrible End, Or An End to the Horror?* (Chicago: RCP Publications, 1983), pp. 133-38.

"not thinking" as a way of characterizing it sharply.

A comrade sent me some tapes of different scholars of religion and religious history lecturing on the Old Testament and the New Testament of the Bible. These were Biblical scholars, but they certainly were not fundamentalists—I don't know if they are atheists or agnostics, but they certainly are not fundamentalists—and I was thinking that (to put it in deliberately extreme and provocative terms) every fundamentalist should be handcuffed to a chair and forced to listen to this discussion of the Bible, because it would completely unhinge their whole view of it. Now that is not ultimately what people need—ultimately and fundamentally, they need the scientific world outlook and methodology of dialectical materialism, they need communist ideology. But the scholars doing the lectures on these tapes are people who are very familiar with the Bible, as familiar as any fundamentalist preacher—or, actually, much more so. But they are also familiar with the whole historical context in which all this is embedded and the whole process that led to these scriptures. People like that need to be marshaled and mobilized, even on their own terms, to fight against these fundamentalists. But even as I'm saying that, I'm wondering: how many communists would *fail to understand* why that is important? So there is a question of training our own people and broader masses in a certain methodology, in order that they can respond to events correctly.

That also was one of Lenin's points in *What Is To Be Done?*: To the degree that people do get trained in this outlook and methodology, it makes a big difference. And it does spread in waves. Here's an example from real life (something people have written us about): a guy in prison struggling with another prisoner over what world outlook to have toward pornography, why it is harmful and oppressive. That has a multiplying effect, when people begin to get something, and they begin to be able to struggle with other people. And people who may never see the outside of a prison, at least until after a revolution, can still play an important role in that revolution, because they can train themselves, politically and ideologically, they can contribute—they can write and they can correspond, they can raise questions, they can raise strategic considerations, they can raise criticisms, and they can struggle with other people and help train them to think like communists—they can make a big contribution even if, unfortunately, they never see the light of day outside the prison again, at least until revolution.

* * * * *

Here let me speak to a methodological point that has been made a number of times in the history of our party and ideological struggles it has waged: As it has been put, many things are true *in the final analysis,* but *there is a long way between here and the final analysis.* Understanding what that means, and the importance of it, is a matter of dialectics and materialism. It's a matter of understanding things this way: If you take a line *to its logical conclusion,* it will amount to X, but that is *not* the same thing as saying that it is *immediately* X. People have to understand the difference there, or they will make all kinds of errors in all kinds of directions—to this side and that side, or both, or to one side and then flipping to the other.

* * * * *

The whole point of principle is that you have to fight for it when it is not easy to do. There is no need for principle if the only time it is applied is when it doesn't matter.

ART AND ARTISTIC CREATION—
SOLID CORE WITH A LOT OF ELASTICITY

With regard to art and artists and their relation to revolution and the revolutionary transformation of the world: Yes, we need "model revolutionary works"[1] and we need collectivity, we need centralized guidance and we need criticism of artistic works. But we also need to let artists go off and do some art and then come back and present what they have done. If it's not good we can tell them honestly what's wrong with it. Maybe they will listen and maybe they won't. We will still—and I'm not a Pollyanna—we will still have to struggle, and in socialist society we'll even have to do some suppression of shit that is really bad and harmful, I'm sorry. Things that actually degrade women, for example. But that's the "easy part." The *hard* part is all the other things that I am emphasizing—the need to apply "solid core with a lot of elasticity" to the sphere of art and culture.

I've read a few parts of (and I'm hoping that soon I'll get to read more of) Bob Dylan's *Chronicles*. Also, accompanying a letter someone recently wrote to me, they sent me the book *Chimes of Freedom: The Politics of Bob Dylan's Art*, by Mike Marqusee, which is very interesting

---

1. "Model works" is a concept that was developed and applied in the Great Proletarian Cultural Revolution in China. These model works were created through a process of involving the input and cooperative efforts of many people in the arts and culture and through centralized guidance and even extensive attention to detail on the part of political leadership from the highest levels of the Chinese Communist Party. These model works not only achieved a high level of revolutionary content but also of artistic excellence. In this discussion, Avakian is speaking to the need for, and importance of, such "model works," but he is also raising certain questions concerning this approach, and in particular the limitations of a one-sided reliance on this kind of approach.

(and I very much appreciate the initiative and generosity of this person in sending this to me). I am now reading that Marqusee book, and while I don't agree with everything I have read so far, it does seem to have a lot of insight. There is a great deal to be learned by grappling with the experience of Bob Dylan—his art and the relation of that to "the left" in a broad sense—there is a lot of positive and negative experience, all the way around, that needs to be learned from. Even some of Dylan's negative and cynical attitudes about the relation between the artist and organized leftist forces involves a lot of things that need to be sorted out and learned from in various ways. You can learn more about what we should expect—and, yes, in a certain sense, demand—from artists, and what we should not.

Dylan goes on and on about how from the time he put out some of these more socially conscious songs, people were coming to him—and maybe he's exaggerating a bit but I still think there is a great deal of truth to it—people were coming to him demanding that he be the "messiah" or that he be the political leader, and he was not a political leader and could not be a political leader. If we had been relating to him, especially if we had been doing this with the correct orientation—and applying the method and principle of "solid core with a lot of elasticity"—we should have been able to do better, much better, than how, it seems, various "leftists" and "leftist groups" related to him. Now, at this point he is where he is, and basically that is what he's going to be—although maybe he'll change again with the changing world—but the point is that there are other people coming forward now, and, yes, we should be correctly having our arm around these people and talking to them about the world—not just their art, talking to them about the world—and struggling with them in a good way about all kinds of things. And then we need to let them go off and do their art.

Would the best of Bob Dylan have been brought forward, if we had led that step by step, especially if we had done this in a narrow, reformist and kind of "workerist" way, and an instrumentalist way, insisting that every artistic creation have some direct and "linear" relation to politics and in particular the immediate political struggles of the day? NO! So, then, does that mean we don't need model works that are really models? No. We do need those things. And there are artists who will be willing to work with us in that way, especially if we work correctly with them. But that is not *all* we need. Life is much more rich—that is the point Lenin was making when he emphasized that the tree of life is much more green than that. Communism does spring from every pore, as Lenin also emphasized; but this won't happen if we "stop up" every pore with a pitiful dogmatist caricature of communism and communist leadership and methods. Even what's not communism can contribute to communism *if* we know how to lead correctly. If we know how to correctly apply "solid core with a lot of elasticity."

Yes, at times it will be messy. And yes, it will be risky. And we should understand that. I didn't use lightly the metaphor of being drawn and quartered,[2] in speaking of what the challenges will be in actually applying the principle of "solid core with a lot of elasticity," not just to the sphere of art *and culture but to the revolutionary process and socialist society as a whole.* That's what it's like if you want to be at the core of this: If you are willing to take the responsibility for being at the core, you are going to have to be willing to and ready to be subjected to those kinds of pressures. That is an important point of orientation, but beyond that, methodologically, you have to be able to correctly apply the outlook and method of communism as it is continually being developed to be able to correctly handle these contradictions. Besides the epistemology discussion, there are important aspects of this that are spoken to in the talk I gave on the dictatorship of the proletariat: *Dictatorship and Democracy, and the Socialist Transition to Communism.*[3]

* * * * *

I have seen discussions by artists in the wake of the 2004 elections talking about how they have to take up the challenge of affecting public opinion—how they have to work collectively together, they have to get to work and even go without sleep. This still essentially represents thinking within the dominant framework, but things are going to be ruptured out of that framework one way or another. We have work to do to rupture them in a good way, and there is a tremendous potential for that. Once we break off the shackles of instrumentalism and economism, there is a tremendous amount that we can do in this sphere of art and culture, working with people in the correct way, and we need to devote the necessary leadership and attention to really doing that. Once again, this is a matter of applying all this methodology that we're

---

2. The metaphor of being drawn and quartered is raised in "Bob Avakian in a Discussion with Comrades on Epistemology: On Knowing and Changing the World," in this volume.

3. *Dictatorship and Democracy, and the Socialist Transition to Communism,* available online at revcom.us and excerpted in the *Revolutionary Worker* from August through December 2004.

talking about, including the solid core with elasticity and all the points I was just speaking to and emphasizing about the different things that we need—not in a narrow utilitarian way but in the broadest sweeping sense of that—what is needed in the sphere of art and culture. So this is another dimension where we need to go to a whole other level. And there is the potential for us to do this, with all different levels of unity with people in these spheres, approaching this in a dynamic way.

EPISTEMOLOGY:
THE DERRIDAS AND THE COMMUNISTS

With regard to philosophers like Derrida, and others in other fields (unfortunately, Derrida is no longer alive, but speaking about him as representative of larger groups of people), it is not that we shouldn't struggle to win these people to communism. But two things: First, there are always going to be people—or, for a long time there will be people—who are *not* going to be communists. That is just an objective reality. So, then, the question is: what about them? Can they contribute anything, do we recognize that they can make contributions? Are they not going to learn important things about reality? For example, can people who are religious who study the history of the Bible teach us anything? Yes. It is not that we shouldn't struggle to win people like this to communism. But for a long time not everybody is going to be won to communism. And then, when we do get to communism, it will be a different dynamic: There will be different schools of thought which will all probably be "post-communist" schools of dialectical materialism.

That brings up the second thing, the other side of it. With the people we *do* win to communism, "solid core with a lot of elasticity"[1]

---

1. Avakian discusses the concept of "solid core with a lot of elasticity" in the talk *Dictatorship and Democracy, and the Socialist Transition to Communism* as follows: "[Y]ou have to have a solid core that firmly grasps and is committed to the strategic objectives and aims and process of the struggle for communism. If you let go of that you are just giving everything back to the capitalists in one form or another, with all the horrors that means. At the same time, if you don't allow for a lot of diversity and people running in all kinds of directions with things, then not only are people going to be building up tremendous resentment against you, but you are also not going to have the rich kind of process out of which the greatest truth and ability to transform reality will emerge." ("A World We Would Want to Live In," *Revolutionary Worker* #1257 [October 31, 2004].)

108 BOB AVAKIAN: OBSERVATIONS ON ART AND CULTURE, SCIENCE AND PHILOSOPHY

takes on a different application, or applies in some different dimensions, on a different level. That is where you want those people to have an *artistic approach* to science, as opposed to a rigid approach to science. Not that you don't want them to be rigorous. There is a difference between being rigorous and being rigid. That is a very important point. You can be rigorously scientific and be artistic at the same time—by which I mean that you explore things from different angles, you try to come at them from different perspectives, you don't get stuck in the rut of always approaching the same problems from the same specific avenues of approach. We want communists especially to be rigorously scientific, but artistic at the same time. That is the point.

Even in the thinking of an individual, there is "solid core with elasticity"—this is true even in an individual's approach to understanding and changing reality, let alone with regard to a party and a whole society. You take up certain core principles, but even there you are not rigid about it. You have to keep looking at reality from different angles—if for no other reason than the fact that you are not going to understand it otherwise. You are not going to get to the deeper level and the inner essence of it without coming at it from a lot of different angles—continuing to go back to the same questions over and over again, with new insights or new accumulated knowledge from many sources.

In some other comments, to be provocative, I used the formulation "the united front under the leadership of the proletariat in the ideological sphere."[2] It is not that we are *not* trying to win people to communism. It would be better if the Derridas were communists—and it would be even better if they were *good* communists, rather than rigid, dogmatic communists. If someone like Derrida were a rigid, dogmatic communist, I don't know if he would have been better than what he was, maybe not. We have had experience with that too. But if someone like that wanted to really be a communist, he'd be better than he was.

Two points in this connection: One, you have to be a *real* communist, in the way I am talking about it; and two, there are going to be others who are going to come along who are *not* going to be communists at any given time. So then I say again: What about them—not just "how can we use them" in the practical struggle, but what about them in terms of how we are going to be able to approach and learn from and

---

2. See the essay "A Scientific Approach to Maoism, A Scientific Approach to Science," in this volume.

assimilate what they come up with even while they are not, or not consistently, applying the communist outlook and methodology?

It struck me—it was over a period of time that it struck me, not one day like a bolt of lightning—that you have all these people in all these spheres whom we now seek to learn from to help us understand reality. It just struck me: Well, why would you think that would stop at some point—when you seize state power or something? Why would you think that would no longer be the case? It didn't make sense to me, epistemologically, that all of a sudden it would no longer be the case that these people could investigate reality and teach us something. Even though we have to apply the dialectical materialist outlook and method to really get the deepest understanding of reality, that doesn't mean that they might not teach us a great deal without applying that outlook (or without applying it consistently and systematically). There is a unity of opposites in that case, too.

I want to re-emphasize the point: It is not that we shouldn't be going out to win them to communism—I'd much rather have these young people you [another comrade in the discussion] are talking about be won to our ideology and be trying to apply it than *not* be won to it. Just because they might do some valuable things while not being communists doesn't mean that it is better for them not to be communists. It is just that, for a whole historical period, there are plenty of people who are not going to be communists, and then what understanding and approach do we have toward them and toward what they are doing?

And yes, under socialism, like under capitalism, there are constraints. Somebody is setting the parameters (the framework and the boundaries or limits). Here is the point: Yes, there are always parameters and somebody is always setting them. And, in this connection, there are a couple of questions: According to what principles? And are there rules to the game—in a relative sense—or is this all arbitrary? There have to be rules to the game that everybody has to adhere to, even though that may be a moving thing that changes, and not something static and forever the same. That is why you have rules and laws and Constitutions, including in socialist society—so people can know what the hell the rules to the game are. How do things get decided and by whom? And through what procedures and institutions do they get decided and implemented? And what and who is accountable to what and whom? Those are things that in socialist society you still have to have. If there are no institutions and instrumentalities like that, then it is just "the party and the masses" and it can be very arbitrary. That was the problem with Lenin's thing about no laws, about dictatorship being unrestricted rule, and specifically rule unrestricted by laws.[3]

Then who is exercising this dictatorship and how do the masses know what the rules are? That is one of the problems. If they don't know what the rules are, how can they be relatively at ease? How can they actually contribute to socialist society and the advance to communism? And how can you actually struggle with people in a good way and toward a good end?

When Lenin was writing there was no experience with the dictatorship of the proletariat, beyond the very short-lived Paris Commune—or, later, he was writing during the very early years of the Soviet republic, when there was still very little experience with this—and nobody thought these dictatorships were going to last very long. That is the other thing—I pointed this out in the talk *Dictatorship and Democracy, and the Socialist Transition to Communism*:[4] When Marx wrote *The Class Struggles in France* and talked about the necessary transit point to the realization of the "four alls" and communism,[5] he didn't have in mind something like 150 years, or more, for that transition. That is a different phenomenon, if you think of this being a few years of transit and then you are off to communism.

The old answer *we* would have given, 25 years ago or more, would have been: "Somebody is always setting the rules, somebody is

---

3. These formulations by Lenin were criticized by Bob Avakian in "Revolutionary Upheavals and the Law: A Contradiction Even in Socialist Society," *Revolutionary Worker* No. 1223 (December 21, 2003) and "Life and Death Situations...The Exercise of Power and the Rights of the People," *Revolutionary Worker* No. 1224 (December 28, 2003). These articles are excerpts from *Getting Over the Two Great Humps: Further Thoughts on Conquering the World*, a talk given by Bob Avakian in the late 1990s.

4. See *Dictatorship and Democracy, and the Socialist Transition to Communism* (excerpted in the *Revolutionary Worker* from August through December 2004 and available online at revcom.us).

5. The "four alls" refers to Marx's statement that the dictatorship of the proletariat is the necessary transit point to the conditions necessary for communism, and specifically to: the abolition of all class distinctions (class distinctions generally); the abolition of all the production relations that give rise to those class distinctions; the abolition of all the social relations that correspond to those production relations; and the revolutionizing of all the ideas that correspond to those relations. (Karl Marx, *The Class Struggles in France, 1848-1850*, in Marx and Engels, *Selected Works*, Vol. 1 [Moscow: Progress Publishers, 1969], p. 282.)

setting the parameters, so don't get too upset. We're better than the bourgeoisie. End of discussion." But there is more to be said and excavated about that too. Even while it is true—both things are true: Somebody *will* be setting the rules and the parameters, and we *are* better than the bourgeoisie. But we won't remain better than the bourgeoisie if that is all we say, and all we think, about it. That is the trick right there.

MARXISM "EMBRACES BUT DOES NOT REPLACE" [1]

Having talked about the principle of "grasp revolution and pro-mote production" and its application to many different spheres and in an overall sense, I want to move to a discussion of the next main point—which is philosophical and methodological questions. I want to begin by focusing on one of these very pithy statements that Mao is sort of famous for making—and the more you grapple with different things that people like Mao, leaders of our class historically, have put forward (and this is especially true of Mao) the more you see how much is real-ly concentrated in some of these very brief statements. Now, as we know, Mao wrote many works—some of them long, some of them short—through the course of his several decades of leadership: he wrote "On Contradiction," "On Practice," "On Protracted War," lots of things on the question of new democracy, and so on. But especially toward the end of his life—partly for reasons of health, but also because this is one of his methods—he would often come out with very short, pithy statements that focused people's attention and unleashed a whole bunch of wrangling.

For example, in what we call "the last great battle" against Deng Xiaoping, in the years '73-'76 (more or less), they were focusing on the question of the dictatorship of the proletariat: why is the dictatorship of the proletariat essential, what is and should be the character of the

---

1. This selection is from the talk *Grasp Revolution, Promote Production: Questions of Outlook and Method, Some Points on the New Situation,* excerpts from which appeared in the *Revolutionary Worker* from November 2002 through March 2003 and are available online at revcom.us. This particular selection was published in *Revolutionary Worker* #1179 (November 22, 2002).

MARXISM "EMBRACES BUT DOES NOT REPLACE"   113

dictatorship of the proletariat, and the whole question of continuing the revolution under the dictatorship of the proletariat. And, instead of writing a whole long essay—which he was probably incapable of doing at that point, but even if he had been, he might very well have used this other method—he posed the question: Why did Lenin say that the dictatorship of the proletariat is essential? Then he followed that up with another sentence: The whole nation should discuss this. And if you think about it [B.A. laughs], that's very pithy. You know, it's like "he's not giving us much guidance"—why did Lenin say that? But what Mao was doing was calling on people to wrangle with that question themselves, to study and to wrestle with the question both in its own right, so to speak—as a matter of principle and theory—but also to situate that in the context of the class struggle that was raging and intensifying at that time in China. So that's kind of a general method that he used at times, and I think there's something to learn from that as far as methods of leadership. Sometimes, posing really important questions is an important way of leading, although sometimes people want answers and we have to give them, so you can't always just pose questions and think you've done your job—if you can just come up with a good question, that's not always enough, but sometimes it's the best method of leadership.

And the statement I want to focus on here is where Mao said (I believe it was in "Talks at the Yenan Forum on Literature and Art"): Marxism embraces but does not replace theories of physics, theories of aesthetics in art, and so on. I want to talk a little bit about what this means and some of the implications and applications of this. This, like everything else, is a unity of opposites, it contains two contradictory aspects: on the one hand, the aspect of "embraces" and, on the other hand, the aspect of "does not replace." Let's go into this a little bit.

What does it mean, and why was he emphasizing, that Marxism does indeed embrace all these different disciplines and fields of inquiry and struggle and so on? Well, of course, partly this is a bit polemical, because there are some people who argued (and, of course, many who still argue) that Marxism does not apply to certain spheres, that it only applies to politics or maybe to philosophy in a general sense. And people like Trotsky in the course of the Soviet Revolution came up with the slogan: in politics, proletarian; in art, bourgeois. In other words, leave the superstructure to tradition, more or less. This was also a big line, of course, in China, and it became a focus of big struggle (and it was not only bourgeois art in that case, but also feudal culture). This became a big focus of struggle in the Cultural Revolution. So, on the one hand, when Mao says Marxism does embrace all these things, this is polemical. He's arguing, yes, Marxism does embrace and is applicable to all these different spheres. And what does that mean? Well, it has to do with the fact that there's objective reality.

Now, I'm going to talk about objective reality a number of times in this talk. It's interesting, I've seen some reports where some of our people, particularly those working among the youth and working among different social and political movements, have observed [*B.A. laughs*] that apparently in some circles, if you use the phrase "objective reality," it's like a code word and right away everybody knows you're associated with our party, because you talk about objective reality and objective truth, instead of identity politics or "my truth" or agnosticism and relativism in general. So, to the degree that's true, it's sort of an interesting commentary on the times and the character of things and where they still have to go and develop—that you're immediately identifiable as being with a certain trend, and our Party in particular, if you talk about objective reality! Nonetheless, there is objective reality, whether anybody likes it or not. And there's no part of reality that is theoretically unknowable, although there will always be parts of reality that are unknown by human beings (and since there's no god, they won't be known by god either). But there is nothing that's inherently unknowable, and there are not ultimately different world outlooks and methodologies for comprehending reality in the fullest and most systematic way—in other words, there is only one world outlook and method that enables you to comprehend reality in the fullest and most systematic way, and that is Marxism (or, today, Marxism-Leninism-Maoism).

Now let me stop here and make a point, however—this is another way in which some of the methodological points I want to stress relate to the fact that life is complex and what we're setting out to do is complex and difficult. It is true—and this is a very important point actually—that while there is no other world outlook and methodology that can enable you to increasingly and more and more deeply and broadly understand reality in a comprehensive and systematic way, that doesn't mean that people who don't have this outlook, or even people who are strongly opposed to it, don't discover some important truths. If you look at people throughout history—people like Darwin, for example—they were far from proletarians. They were not Marxists. In fact, I heard that Marx actually wanted to dedicate *Capital* to Darwin, and Darwin declined. Apparently, he didn't want to be associated with Marx in that way. But the fact remains: Darwin wasn't a Marxist, yet he discovered a very important—and, ironically and amazingly, a still very contentious—truth.

So this is another contradictory aspect of reality we have to understand: on the one hand, Marxism is the only world outlook and methodology that enables you to thoroughly and systematically and in a comprehensive way engage and learn more and more deeply about reality; but it isn't true that people who don't have the Marxist outlook and methodology, or are even opposed to it, cannot discover important truths. There's not only Darwin but Einstein and many other people throughout history, going back even before Marxism was brought into being. Obviously, such people have discovered many important truths, and that will continue to be the case, even in the socialist transition period—this is a very important point to understand or we'll make some very serious errors in the direction of bureaucratism, dogmatism, and some of the errors that we associate, for example, with Stalin.

But, with all that, it is true that Marxism embraces all these spheres. It embraces all of reality. It is a world outlook and methodology that can and should be applied to every sphere of reality in order to grasp it most deeply as it actually is and as it's actually moving and changing, in its motion and development. So that speaks to the "embraces" aspect. But what about the "does not replace" aspect?

The Particularity of Contradiction

This has to do with something Mao emphasized in "On Contradiction," which is the particularity of contradiction. Reality doesn't exist as an abstraction or in general. Material reality exists in the form of particular forms of matter in motion at any given time, although all particular forms are always coming into being and going out of being and undergoing transformation while they exist. So this is another important unity of opposites to grasp. But what I want to emphasize right here is the particularity of contradiction. Mao pointed out in the same essay, "On Contradiction," that qualitatively different contradictions are resolved by qualitatively different means. For example, colonial oppression is resolved by national wars or the struggle for national liberation. The struggle between the bourgeoisie and the proletariat is resolved by the class struggle. The requirements of production are resolved by carrying out production, although once again the complexity of life is that, just as soon as you do that, you enter into relations of production, and the sphere of production interpenetrates closely with, is a unity of opposites with, those relations of production and with the struggle over them. So this again is the complexity of reality, but at the same time reality does exist in relatively—*relatively*—discrete forms. Otherwise, it would be impossible to distinguish one thing from another. And, more fundamentally, matter would not actually exist if it all were just some sort of undifferentiated blob—or, to put it another way, matter could not exist in that mode—it does not exist in that mode because of the very nature of matter. (Whether there could have developed another kind of matter that existed in different ways than matter as it has actually developed is in fact a very interesting question that has to do with various fields of science, and the philosophy of science; but that is beyond the scope of what I am speaking to here. The essential point here is that matter actually does exist in different, relatively discrete forms—it has particularity, relatively.)

So it is necessary, in order to actually make progress in, and carry out transformation in, any particular sphere or discipline or activity, to go deeply into the particularity of contradiction. If people are trying to do something, for instance, in the sphere of physics or some of the other sciences—wrestling, for example, with problems concerning the origin of the known universe—and we send a comrade to meet with a group of scientists wrangling with this and our comrade says, "What's the problem? Marxism-Leninism-Maoism—that's the answer"—well, that's not going to be very satisfactory, and it's actually not going to supply the answer. If we all memorize quotations—or let's say we all memorize everything that Marx, Engels, Lenin, Stalin, and Mao said about physics—that is not going to supply the answer that's needed to these kinds of vexing and at the same time very exhilarating questions, and it's not going to contribute positively to the wrangling about questions having to do with the nature of matter and with the transformation of matter, with the origins of the known universe, etc. Not only coming in and just doing something as crude as reciting all the quotations from all the great Marxist "classics" about this particular sphere, but also just coming in and saying, "Dialectical materialism teaches us that everything is matter in motion, and that motion is absolute while temporary forms of stability of matter are secondary and partial"—well, that's true, but what the hell does that have to do with the particular problems? Actually, it does have to do with them, but you have to apply this concretely. You have to actually go deeply into the particularity of contradiction that you're confronting, into the particular sphere or discipline, or the particular problem within that sphere or discipline, and really wrestle with that.

And this has to do with the whole principle of combining the masses with the experts, with the principle of red and expert, of red leading expert, the non-professional leading the professional. That doesn't mean that people who don't know anything about a sphere come in and issue orders to people who do; or that people come into a sphere and, as soon as someone raises something that contradicts what we believe to be true at a given time, you simply bring down the official line, slam the door shut, and close off debate. Now, there have been tendencies in the history of our movement to do this, but this is something we have to learn from by negative example. If we are really going to carry out everything we're seeking to carry out historically, we're going to have to rupture with such methods. We're going to have to learn how to go deeply into things.

For example, there is a role for experts in relation to our ability to lead in various spheres, and such experts can be an important link when they're won over to our world outlook and methodology. They can be a link between the Party (and the vanguard forces in general) and others who are expert in a particular sphere. You have to have people who are both expert in a sphere and also consciously seeking to apply the "embrace" principle, consciously seeking to apply our world outlook and methodology. Otherwise, it's going to be very difficult to lead. And if you don't know anything about a sphere, it's impossible ultimately to lead other than by the most commandist and bureaucratic methods—which everyone is going to rebel against, openly or secretly, and the results are going to be very undesirable in terms of our strategic goals, because after all, despite what the anarchists might say or think, we're not just trying to grab power in order to exercise power over the people. We're trying to carry out a world-historic transformation in which the masses will ultimately emancipate themselves and achieve a classless society and a world of freely associating human beings. That's a tall order, as the saying goes—that's a tremendously great challenge—and it can't be accomplished by those kinds of bureaucratic methods.

So, again, you can err in one direction or the other (or one and then the other, or some combination of them). You can forget the "embraces" part and get lost in a particular sphere and think that our basic principles have nothing to do with this, or that this has nothing to do with our strategic objectives. You can fall into tailing spontaneity, tailing the masses, pragmatism, losing sight of the relation between the particular and the universal—that is, between a particular arena of activity or struggle and our ultimate goal of achieving communism, and between learning about one particular sphere and increasing the store of knowledge of humanity as a whole. So you can forget the "embraces" aspect and forget the universal in that sense.

On the other hand (and this is what I was just speaking to) you can also lose sight of the particular, the "does not replace" aspect. That's what Mao means with "does not replace": he means you can't just have Marxist principles in a general or abstract sense. You have to apply them. You have to apply them in a living way, and you have to learn from others in the course of applying them and apply the mass line in the spheres of science, and so on, in order to be able to correctly learn and lead. So, again, these errors can go on one side or the other: forgetting the universal, forgetting the broad strategic objectives, forgetting the "embraces"; or, on the other hand, forgetting the particularity of contradiction. You can fall into forgetting the "does not replace." You can fall into forgetting the need to actually go deeply into a sphere, to immerse yourself in a certain sense, but immerse yourself without losing the other aspect, without losing the sense of the universal, without losing the sense of the strategic, without losing the aspect of "embraces." So the difficult task is to immerse yourself to really deal with the particularity of contradiction, to learn in a particular sphere, while overall leading and in order to lead in the best way; but also to keep in mind the universal, keep in mind the "embraces."

This is a very crucial principle that Mao concentrated, it is very dialectical in reflecting reality, and it requires a tremendous amount of continual work and summation to be able to apply this correctly, because again you can veer one way or the other, or you can find some sort of worst of all worlds combination of halfway being universal and halfway dealing with the particular, but not really applying either aspect correctly, so that you end up with a pragmatic mush. These are all the kinds of errors which everyone who has set out to do what we're setting out to do is familiar with [*B.A. laughs*] and has committed on more than one or a few occasions. But there's no way to correct that, no way to do the right thing, except to continually grapple with these principles and how they apply, and to keep coming back to the overall and the universal, but then go back in turn to the particular...and on and on—which parallels in a certain sense the ongoing theory-practice-theory dialectic.

Working with Ideas

Now, connected with this is a sort of fascinating point in an article by Ardea Skybreak (in the *RW*) on "Working with Ideas."[2] This is something to ponder and wrangle with in a broad and an open-ended way, which in fact is in line with the substance and spirit of that article. It's the following argument:

"Failing to recognize the degree to which it is important to 'let the reins go a bit' in the unfolding of intellectual work will result in a suffocating and stifling bureaucratized atmosphere, and the production of a very few slowly and laboriously crafted, overly labor and energy intensive, good works. Many other works will never be undertaken at all, and in fact, few intellectuals will ever want to work under such energy and morale sapping strictures, and those few good works that do get produced may well contain many good points and minutely calibrated precisions, but they will also be stripped of much of life, humor, artistry, and especially of those thought-provoking tangents and ruminations which are the stuff on which further intellectual exchange and dialogue tends to build."

This is actually raising a very important point. It has to do with what I was saying earlier about the Mensheviks and their methodology, or the revisionists in China: "What's this got to do with carrying out production? This is just another one of these diversions from the task at hand. Why do we need to talk about philosophy or world history or, God forbid, singing and dancing? What does that have to do with what's immediately on our agenda?" Now, we do have to pay attention to our agenda. There are things we're trying to accomplish in the world, and if we don't accomplish them, it's not good. We're engaged in a very intense class struggle. But this goes back to the "grasp/promote" principle, with which I introduced this talk, and I think what's being gotten at, in this quote from this Ardea Skybreak article, is really something to think about and wrestle with—what it is attempting to focus on and wrangle with is a very important question.

And, to expand a little bit on this point, it's interesting to think about the relation of what's said there in that Skybreak article to certain criticisms that have been raised with regard to the sphere of art and culture and how it came to be handled in China after a certain point in the

---

2. "Working with Ideas and Searching for Truth: A Reflection on Revolutionary Leadership and the Intellectual Process," *Revolutionary Worker* #1144 (March 24, 2002), available online at revcom.us.

Cultural Revolution. One of the things that has been pointed out is that a tremendous amount of work and collective effort and struggle and attention to minute detail actually went into producing the model cultural works that came forward through the Cultural Revolution, because this wasn't a matter of bringing something new into being in a vacuum—they were going up against and struggling every step of the way against the old and against the attempt to stifle and suffocate these model works and to uphold tradition in opposition to them. So there was a tremendous amount of work that was concentrated on this, that had to be concentrated on this. And even our enemies have, ironically, had to acknowledge that these works, whatever they think of them politically (and they don't like them politically and ideologically, obviously), were tremendous artistic creations and represented something new in the sphere of art.

I remember reading not too long ago (within the last year or so, I think) an article in the *New York Times* where they acknowledged this. This article mentioned how in China people still talk about these works that came forward then, model works of the Cultural Revolution, and what tremendous achievements they were. And I specifically remember that there was one guy they quoted who worked on these model works who was refreshingly and excitingly unrepentant. He not only upheld those works but raised pointedly: "How many works of a high artistic level have these clowns in power now brought forward?" I'm paraphrasing, but that was the essence of what he said. This is reflecting the fact that it's not easy to bring forward works like these model works, and we should not lose sight of the fact that these are tremendous achievements of our class and of its vanguard leadership. These were really new things, world-historical new things, that were brought into being.

At the same time—and I'm not trying to pass a verdict on this, I'm raising it as a question that I think is worth not only pondering but looking into further and wrestling with in terms of its specificity but also in terms of some of the broader questions it raises that I'm trying to point to and promote some wrangling around—the criticism has been made that, after a certain point, things around these model works turned into their opposite (or bringing forward new works turned into its opposite) to a certain degree and in a certain sense, because nothing could be promoted other than these model works, and everything that people attempted to create (this is the criticism that was raised) had to be gone over with the same degree of laborious and fine-tuned and calibrated attention (to refer again to the Skybreak article) that the model works had required in order to be brought into being. This is an interesting question. As I said, I'm not trying to pass a verdict on whether this is a valid criticism, but it is something that I think is definitely worth looking into, investigating, struggling over, wrangling with—trying to learn more about it, and about the larger implications of whatever the truth of this is.

Levels of Reality

I will say that, as a general principle, if you try to put the same amount of attention to everything as you put to certain things you're trying to bring forward as concentrated models, you're going to stifle and suffocate a lot of effort and initiative on the part of people. Everything can't be a model work, and everything can't be and shouldn't be the result of that level of attention, concentration, and leadership. To my understanding, things like even questions of "stage management" of these model operas—for example, where different props were placed and all those kinds of questions—were ultimately decided, although others were involved, at a very high level of leadership. There was a tremendous amount of attention to detail. And once again, in a general sense, I would say that that's not a very good method—that's not going to allow enough initiative for people, if everything (even where you put a certain prop) has to go up to the very highest level to be discussed and evaluated and approved or not approved. If it's a decision at a Central Committee level or Politburo level whether this tree is here or six inches away, that is obviously going to stifle a lot of initiative, at least if that's a general method. But again, reality is very complicated and these works weren't being brought forward in a vacuum; they were being brought forward in the course of very intense struggle where people were using any shortcomings that could be found in them to attack the whole thing, not just a particular work—a particular ballet or Peking Opera, *The Red Detachment of Women* or the redoing of *White-Haired Girl* or whatever—but the model works as a whole and the whole breakthrough in the arena of culture.

So it's a very complicated question how you handle this, and sometimes things can be very innocent and sometimes they're not—it depends on the specific condition, time, and place. Take, for example, things that kicked off the Cultural Revolution.

There was this well-known artistic work in China, *Hai Jui Dis-*

missed from Office, and, as I recall, someone wrote a review of this. The play was just a thinly veiled form (what later came to be known as the Lin Biao and Confucius method, the Aesopian indirect method) of attacking Mao by analogy. This was at a crucial point in the Chinese revolution; and Mao, being rather astute and not obtuse, picked this up right away and wrote an essay or a commentary pointing this out and calling on people to do criticism and struggle around this. At other times, Mao would have said, and did say, "Oh, you know, let that go." Somebody makes a comment that, yes, if you took it and tracked it down to its ultimate logical conclusion, would be very bad. But so what? It's a more or less innocent—or, if not so innocent, harmless— comment in the particular context. But, in other contexts, it's not so innocent or so harmless. Even subtle, little fine nuances of things can have tremendous meaning in certain contexts, while in other contexts they have almost no meaning at all.

So, there again is the particularity of contradiction, and there's the matter of levels. What are we dealing with here? But, along with the particularity of contradiction, there's the relation between the particular and the universal. Again, what are we dealing with here? What is the particularity? You have to know it and understand it. What does it have to do with larger questions of the class struggle, for example—which are the universal in that context. As Mao pointed out in "On Contradiction," what's particular in one context is universal in another, and vice versa.

In other words, if you're fighting a war, then taking that war as a whole, the war situation as a whole is the universal; and any particular campaign within that war can be regarded as the particular in relation to that universal. But, in turn, if you take that particular campaign and look at it, and examine it internally, so to speak, then that campaign becomes the universal, and any particular battle within that campaign is the particular. Then if you go to the next level and take that battle, and examine it internally so to speak, that becomes the universal, and particular tactics in that battle—blocking tactics or tactical offensives or whatever—become the particular...and so on, and so on, and so on. Again, what makes reality so complex and our work so difficult is that you have to distinguish between what levels you're dealing on, what's the particular and what's the universal, and what's the relationship in turn between whatever you're determining to be universal in that context and the universal on a larger and broader scale. For example, going back to the example I was just using, a war as a whole is a universal with regard to that war; but, with regard to your revolutionary objectives as a whole, it's a particular. So this is the kind of dialectical thinking and methodology that we have to apply.

Getting back to the particular thing I was talking about, in the sphere of art and culture, even such things as where stage props are situated *could* be a big deal—it could be a very important particular that touches on the whole universal—or it could be not very important, and even if people are up to a lot of skullduggery and evil intent with moving it six inches to the left or the right, maybe you'd just go, "Eh, who cares? Let's not fight over that."

This has to do with a statement that was attributed to Mao by the revisionists who seized power in China shortly after Mao's death. (And again it's important to keep in mind, with such statements in general, that we don't really have any way to authenticate them—that is, statements that are attributed to Mao after he's dead and the coup has taken place, when these revisionists are in power and they can, in the short run, craft things the way they want to, more or less. So we have to try to critically evaluate these things.) In *GO&GS* (*Great Objectives and Grand Strategy*)[3] I referred to one of these statements attributed to Mao, where he talks about the treatment of intellectuals (and I'm going to come back to that in a little bit).

But another thing that was interesting—and this involves the statement attributed to Mao that I want to focus on here—was that there was this conference on developing agriculture and learning from a model area, Dazhai, in agriculture (in 1975 I believe), where Hua Guofeng and others spoke (Hua Guofeng would be, a year later, the leader of the coup which put an end to socialism in China, and then he in turn was dumped from high office after Deng Xiaoping came back fully to power and Hua Guofeng was no longer needed by the top revisionists). According to what was said after the coup, the Gang of Four attacked Hua Guofeng's speech at that conference and criticized a lot of the conference. And, supposedly, in commenting on their criticisms, Mao made the remark which was variously translated as "Shit, wide of the mark!" or "Barking up the wrong tree."

Now, let's accept that at face value in order to illustrate a point

---

3. *Great Objectives and Grand Strategy* is an unpublished work by Bob Avakian; excerpts from it have been published in the *Revolutionary Worker* #1127 through 1142, November 18, 2001 through March 10, 2002. They are available online at revcom.us.

that I'm trying to emphasize here: even if Mao said that, that doesn't necessarily mean that he thought the substance of their criticisms was wrong. It might have meant instead: look, this is not the way to focus the class struggle right now, because you're going to confuse things. You're going to mix up the main enemy with secondary enemies or middle forces. Many people may be enthusiastic for this conference, and you're going to confuse them. You're going to make them think you're down on the effort to make advances and leaps in agriculture. Plus there are other questions around which the class struggle is much more clearly crystallizing, and we should keep our attention focused on that.

Now, again, this is hypothetical to a large degree because of the source of this and the context in which these quotes came out. But nonetheless, the principle applies that sometimes things are worth really pursuing down to the most minute detail, and on many other occasions this is not the case and it's much better to let things go. Mao pointed out that there is a unity of opposites between leadership and centralism, on the one hand, and laissez-faire on the other hand. He said there is a certain role for laissez-faire—not laissez-faire capitalism but laissez-faire in a more general sense. But again, as reality is complicated, laissez-faire can lead to laissez-faire capitalism if it's not correctly handled in relation to our overall objectives.

Sorting Things Out

A certain theme is obviously being repeatedly emphasized here— that all this is complex and difficult. I'm not saying that to spread pessimism and defeatism or demoralization, not at all, but just to emphasize that we can learn and master these things—in an ongoing way and not in some absolute sense—but it takes work. It takes struggle. It requires applying the universal, taking up the "embraces" aspect, as well as getting into the particularity of contradiction and distinguishing between different levels and correctly handling the dialectical relationship between different levels. This is a question that is being wrestled with in the part of the Skybreak article that I cited. It's discussing the intellectual sphere in particular—working with ideas—but there's a way in which this also applies to the artistic sphere. And there is the question: is there even some validity to some of the criticisms that have been raised with regard to the Cultural Revolution—that if you insist on paying the same amount of minute calibrated attention to more than just a few things, you're going to stifle a lot of initiative; and if people work "for you" it's going to be working *for* you, and they're going to work without enthusiasm and initiative, they're not really going to be unleashed.

In any case, beyond that particular criticism, there is the more general principle that I've been speaking to, concerning when we should, and when we should not, pay great attention to things, even to minute details of things. This is something that we should keep in mind, and it applies to many different spheres—not just to the intellectual and artistic spheres, although it does apply in important ways there. Sometimes we have to pay a lot of attention and really see each step through. There are times like that, and if we don't recognize that, we're not going to achieve a lot of our objectives and the masses are not going to be happy with us, and for good reason, because sometimes they need that level of attention and leadership from us—going back and forth with them, not in a commandist sense but by applying the mass line. They need us to pay that much attention especially where there are tremendously difficult new things that are being brought into being, or struggles that are being waged at close quarters with the enemy. Other times we're going to drive them crazy if we do that—and drive them away—because they need to be able to go out and take some initiative. At those times, the masses need us to *not* pay such close attention to detail, and not only is it necessary to give them more room for their own initiative, but it's also necessary to let different flowers bloom and schools of thought contend (to use that phrase), to let different experience accumulate in order to sift through and get the richest synthesis at a certain crucial point. So there's another unity of opposites that we have to learn how to handle.

And, going back to the intellectual sphere, in *GO&GS* I referred to this comment about Duhring. This is another one of these quotes that, as I pointed out, is attributed to Mao in circumstances in which we have no way of verifying whether it's authentic or not. But just to take it up and deal with the principle that it's touching on (and, for the purposes of our own thinking and our own wrangling with these questions, let's just assume for the moment that Mao did say this): he made a comment to the effect that there was too much stifling of the intellectual atmosphere, it wasn't a conducive atmosphere for intellectual work, inquiry, and wrangling, and he made the point (this was another one of his typical ways of going at things) that even Engels protested when Duhring was deprived of his seat in the university.

Everybody knows that Engels wrote this whole long polemic *Anti-*

Duhring (and it has been pointed out that Engels thereby made Duhring much more famous than he would have been otherwise) but even though Engels ripped into Duhring on many different levels—politically, as well as with regard to political economy, methodologically and philosophically in general—when the reactionary German authorities cracked down on Duhring, Engels was part of the people who protested this. What Mao is getting at is something he spoke to in "On the Correct Handling of Contradictions among the People"—and again this has to do with the particularity of contradiction and the principle of "embraces but does not replace"—that the ideological sphere is different than other spheres and it's particularly harmful in the ideological sphere, broadly understood, to apply crude methods. It's always bad to apply crude and crudely coercive methods, but it's particularly harmful in the ideological sphere, where things have to be grappled with and the truth has to be arrived at through a complex process of wrangling, and where oftentimes correct ideas are in the hands of a minority and don't appear, even to good people, to be true. So, again, it's particularly important not to handle things crudely in that sphere.

In other words, Mao is saying: we shouldn't act like the reactionary German authorities and suppress every intellectual whose ideas or theories we don't agree with. We have to wrestle those things out through ideological struggle.

If people are actually counter-revolutionary and engage in counter-revolutionary political activity against the dictatorship of the proletariat, and especially if they take that to the point of organizing attempts to overthrow the proletarian dictatorship, that's one thing. But if they merely express backward or even reactionary ideas, that's another thing.

This gets back to the point I was making earlier about how even people who have reactionary political views and even methodology that's radically different from ours can still come up with important aspects of truth. And if we lose sight of the particularity of contradiction—if we take the fact that these people are politically and maybe even ideologically reactionary and confuse that with the particularity of whatever sphere of knowledge they're dealing with, and we assume that automatically they are bound to be wrong about this or that sphere of science or medicine or whatever, simply because they're generally, or maybe even extremely, reactionary ideologically and politically—we're going to make all kinds of mistakes. This is the point Mao was getting at. And this does require us to sort things out, to see things on different levels, and not to be reductionist in our thinking.

What do I mean here by reductionist? Well, here you have someone whose overall world outlook and methodology and political stand is reactionary, so you conclude that this is going to apply to everything—you reduce everything to this one aspect, or one level—you "mash" everything together, so that everything they say about everything is going to be wrong. Even if they get up and say, "The sun came up this morning," they're bound to be wrong because they are reactionary ideologically and politically. No. Everything has to be examined in its own right to determine if it's true or false. As Mao said in another work, we should take a sniff at everything and decide whether to boycott it or support it.

Now it's true, and this also makes it complex, that if you are politically and ideologically reactionary, if your methodology is opposed to the correct methodology—or even different from it—then, ultimately, or in the final analysis, this is going to show up not only in your methodology in general but also in your analysis of any particular thing. But, as we used to say—including in the course of the struggle around what stand to take on China—between here and the final analysis there is often a great deal. If you "mash" and reduce everything down to what's true in the final analysis, you'll make a lot of mistakes.

Going back even further, we pointed this out emphatically in the polemics we wrote against PL (Progressive Labor Party), which at a certain point came out and said that all nationalism is reactionary. This is obviously one of the most important questions for the whole revolutionary process worldwide but also in a particularly concentrated way in the U.S.: the relation between the national question and the class question (or the class struggle and ultimately the achievement of socialism and communism) is a very complex and obviously pivotal and crucial question. We have, of necessity, spent a great deal of time investigating and grappling with this question, this relation, and in a certain period—in the period of a few years leading up to the formation of the Party—there was a tremendous amount of attention and struggle devoted to this.

Many things were written, polemics back and forth, on this question of how to correctly understand the national question, or different national questions, and their relation to the proletarian revolution overall.[4] PL adopted the position that all nationalism is reactionary, and we had to bring out that there are different kinds of nationalism. There is the nationalism of the oppressor nation (the European-American nation in the U.S., for example) and there's the nationalism of oppressed peoples and nations—which is very different, especially in its political effect. So we had to point out that, yes, in the final analysis, ideologically, all nationalism is bourgeois—it's a reflection of the bourgeois world outlook—but that's true in the final analysis. It doesn't mean that in every particular instance, or even in a struggle overall, such nationalism can only play a reactionary role because in the final analysis the bourgeoisie is a reactionary class. We had to get into all of the particularities there. We had to get into the different levels of reality, different levels of matter in motion, different levels of the association of matter, if you want to put it that way; we had to distinguish different stages and different levels of things and correctly assess and handle the relation between the particular and the universal.

Now, on the other hand, we had to struggle against people whom (drawing from the history of the Russian Revolution) we came to call Bundists, within our own ranks and more broadly in the revolutionary movement of that time, in particular the BWC (the Black Workers Congress) and the PRRWO (the Puerto Rican Revolutionary Workers Organization, which emerged from the Young Lords Party). They were basically arguing that the nationalism of an oppressed people or nation is bound to be revolutionary and that revolutionary nationalism is essentially identical with proletarian ideology. And we came up with a formulation that really infuriated them [B.A. laughs], partly because it was sort of deliberately provocative: we said all nationalism is...nationalism, and all nationalism is ultimately bourgeois ideologically. So then they accused us of being just like PL. PL said all nationalism is reactionary, and we said all nationalism is bourgeois, ideologically. Are those the same thing? No—precisely because we drew a distinction, including in these polemics, between world outlook—the character of nationalism as an ideology, as a world view—and the application of that ideology in different circumstances. And we correctly emphasized (as we did in the struggle against PL) that, in the case of an oppressed people, national-

---

4. The polemics referred to here were published in *Red Papers 5: National Liberation and Proletarian Revolution in the U.S.* and *Red Papers 6: Build the Leadership of the Proletariat and Its Party*, by the Revolutionary Union in 1972 and 1974, respectively.

ism, even though it's ultimately bourgeois *ideologically*, can assume a progressive and even a revolutionary expression *politically*, but ultimately it's not going to be able to lead people all the way to liberation—even to national liberation, let alone to complete social emancipation, in other words, the elimination of all class distinctions and oppressive social divisions.

Here again, you have to look at the particularity of contradiction and correctly handle the relation between the particular and the universal, between the immediate and the final analysis, and not crush together all the different levels. This is another illustration of the fact that there are no "magic" formulae, or sing-songy formulas that you can memorize, that are going to tell you exactly what to do in every situation. That's the complexity of reality. And you can't deal with all this, other than by applying both the "embraces" and the "does not replace"; by dealing both with the universal and what's true in the final analysis, on the one hand, and with the particularity of contradiction and with different levels and how something is assuming an expression at a given time, on the other hand.

To turn again to the example of nationalism, politically there are many forms of nationalism which propel people into motion and into struggle with which we're going to have to and must seek to unite. At the same time, we can't tail that. We can't think that that's going to ultimately lead to where things need to go. The fact that nationalism is bourgeois ideology *is* going to ultimately have its effects. But, again, what's true ultimately or in the final analysis is not the same thing as what's immediately true or true in any particular set of circumstances. So sorting these things out—correctly handling the relation between them and correctly forging (and reforging in the course of ongoing reality and practice) the necessary synthesis—is not easy. But just as it's difficult, it's also crucial, it's key to being able to make advances through all the twists and turns.

So, in getting back to what Mao said about the intellectual sphere, the sphere of ideas, he was stressing: We cannot handle things in a crude manner there, and we cannot mix up qualitatively different contradictions. We cannot treat the ideological sphere as exactly the same as the political. And we cannot confuse the fact that someone may be backward, even reactionary, in terms of their political stand, or their ideology, with whether or not they have any truth in their hands and whether or not there is any role they can play in our arriving at a deeper understanding of a particular aspect of reality and our understanding of reality as a whole—which is dialectically related to transforming it.

There is the particularity of contradiction. There are different levels of matter in motion. There is a need to distinguish and correctly handle these contradictions, to distinguish between the particular and the universal and between different kinds of matter in motion, which exist in relatively discrete forms, and between different levels of matter in motion (or different aggregations or associations of matter in motion which exist on different levels). That's one point I have been repeatedly returning to and emphasizing, because it's really important to focus on this and wrestle with it, both on the level of conception and in terms of how, without being narrow and pragmatic, this applies to many different spheres.

WE CAN'T KNOW EVERYTHING—
SO WE SHOULD BE GOOD AT LEARNING [1]

The next point I want to speak to is something that was brought out in the anarchism series[2] I wrote about five years ago (which appeared in the *RW* at that time). This was a critique of and a polemic in certain ways against the anarchist outlook and different political and programmatic expressions of anarchism. But one of the things that was stressed there was this: the fact that we are making a critique of anarchism and that we have very sharp differences with the anarchists does not at all mean that anarchists cannot play a positive role in the revolutionary struggle overall—some of them can and do, at least at various times and in various aspects. Again, this has to be determined concretely.

It was someone with essentially anarchist politics who, in the course of the Russian Revolution, shot Lenin in the head, which had a lot to do with his developing the strokes and disease that killed him, not that much later. So, obviously [*B.A. laughs*] out of anarchist motivation, people can do very bad things. But that doesn't mean that overall we should dismiss the anarchists as being inevitably (or in the final analysis even) in the camp of counterrevolution; we shouldn't think

---

1. This selection is from the talk *Grasp Revolution, Promote Production: Questions of Outlook and Method, Some Points on the New Situation*, excerpts from which appeared in the *Revolutionary Worker* from November 2002 through March 2003 and are available online at revcom.us. This particular selection was published in *Revolutionary Worker* #1181 (December 29, 2002).

2. The five-part series "MLM vs. Anarchism" appeared in *Revolutionary Worker* #919-923, August 17 through September 14, 1997 and is available online at revcom.us.

that, at any given time, they can't play a very positive role in many ways (and this applies especially now).

As opposed to that, we should recognize the need to have a relationship of unity-struggle-unity, not tailing but also not dismissing, or treating antagonistically, at least many of the various anarchist trends and people who are drawn to them. This is something that was emphasized in that series, and then it went on to make the point, not only in regard to anarchists specifically but more generally, that at any given time, both before and after the seizure of power, the vanguard party has to, by definition and as part of its role, focus on certain key areas or arenas or struggles in society, and it cannot be paying attention to everything, even every important thing that's going on in society and the world as a whole. We have to focus on certain key things in order to actually advance the class struggle and, by definition, our concentrating there means that we're not paying attention, or not as much attention, to other things, and specifically not paying as much attention to them as some other forces. So we may not know as much about a particular sphere at any given time as others in society, anarchists or other forces.

And once again, because we are the vanguard ideologically and politically and have that role and responsibility in an overall sense, we can't assume—again it's the "embraces but does not replace" principle[3]—we can't assume this translates into our "automatically" knowing more about everything than everybody else—or, if not automatically, then with just a little effort, we will very quickly know more than everybody else about everything. That's completely wrong. And this is an error that's been made in the history of our movement, just as errors have been made in making a leap to saying that, because someone's outlook may be ultimately reactionary politically and ideologically, that means they're incapable of arriving at any important truth. It's also been assumed sometimes, on the other side of it, that because we're the political and ideological vanguard, this means that, even without turning our attention—or at least as soon as we turn our attention—to a sphere, we'll automatically know more than everybody else about this.

In thinking about this point, I was recalling when, way back in 1979, I did a speaking tour around the country and I went to a college

---

3. This principle was the subject of much of the previous excerpt in this series, "Marxism 'Embraces But Does Not Replace'," which is the previous selection in this volume.

campus (I don't remember exactly where) and I was interviewed by someone on the college radio station. We got to talking about the punk phenomenon, which was sort of a relatively new phenomenon at that time. And this person became very animated and angry and was saying, "Here you go again, you communists, you always want to take credit for everything and pretend that everything was your invention or your creation! You didn't create the punk phenomenon, but now you're coming around talking about this punk phenomenon as if it's this great thing and you're all behind it." And I said, "No, no, no, no. [*B.A. laughs*] You're missing the point. The point is not that we created it. The point is that there are many things in society, including this punk phenomenon, which are brought forward by many different people; we couldn't possibly bring everything new and positive into being. The punk phenomenon has some negative aspects, but it also has some very positive ones, and our role is not to try to create everything or to have everything tightly under our control, but to try to identify things that are positive and to unite with them while struggling and trying to help them advance even more and become even more fully positive."

But this was something sort of new to him. This person assumed that, if we were talking positively about something, we were trying to "take credit" for it and act as if it were our creation. And if, in fact, we were doing that, then the criticism would definitely be justified, because that's not the way reality works.

Many different new things, positive and negative, are going to be brought into being not only by us but by other people, and it's a question of how do we view and relate to them, how do we unite with them but also struggle with them, how do we sift through and help others sift through and synthesize what's correct and progressive and even revolutionary within them and cast off those things that are the opposite, that are backward or are incorrect. This is in essence another application, or another aspect of applying, the mass line. And that's what we're about. We couldn't possibly think that everything that's new and positive is going to be brought into being by us, or that we're going to understand more about everything in society and the world and nature and history than everybody else.

Learning to Take Criticism

And sometimes, even with things that we do "specialize" in—that we are focusing our attention on—other people standing outside of what we're doing, who don't have the same focussed attention on it, may be able to see things about this that we don't see, may be able to understand things about that sphere in general, or about our work in that sphere and what conclusions we're drawing, that may be very important. We should always listen to that and learn from that, even when it's raised in the absolutely worst spirit (and, of course, it's more welcome and easier to listen to when it's raised in a good spirit). Mao said we should toughen our skin: we should learn to take criticism; we should learn to look for what's true and to sift through and come to a synthesis about things that are even raised in the most nasty way. I mean, you can struggle with people about their methods and how they raise things, but not by way of dismissing what they're raising or confusing the two different questions. *What* they raise is one question, one particularity; the *way* they raise it is another question, another particularity. While they're obviously interrelated, they're also separate. And we have to always have an open mind.

In fact, we should always be interrogating ourselves as well as listening to "interrogation" from others. There's a saying that defeated armies learn well. Well, one of the things we're going to have to learn to apply is the principle that victorious armies (of course I'm speaking metaphorically here and not just literally) should also learn well. In other words, in many ways it's easier to listen when you're having trouble, easier to accept criticism when you're not doing very well. It's harder to be open to criticism when you're doing well. Triumphalism sets in. You don't want to hear it: "What do you know?" There was a whole thing in the course of the Cultural Revolution in China where they talked about bourgeois democrats in the Chinese party leadership—long-time veterans—who turned into capitalist roaders. These people would scoff and say to the red guards and other new comrades, "Capitalist roader, what do you know, you punk? I was marching over snow-capped mountains before you were born, and sloshing through the marshes—we lost 90% of our army, we fought a battle or more every day, we covered over 5,000 miles in the Long March. What were you doing then? [*B.A. laughs*] You weren't even alive. You have it soft—you were born in the new society. What do you know about revolutionary struggle and going up against odds?"

Well, that's incorrect. I mean, it's true that they did all those things, but that doesn't make you immune from making errors or even going revisionist, and it doesn't mean that you have a right to reject—or should adopt the attitude of rejecting—criticism out of hand or creating an atmosphere in which people don't feel easy about raising criticism, no matter how many contributions you've made and no matter how much success you've been a part of. In fact, it's especially important when you're being (or have been) successful to listen to others who have criticisms and even to interrogate yourself, constantly. Marx talked about how the proletarian revolution has to constantly pick itself up and shake off the dust and go forward again, after we suffer setbacks and defeats. Well, we also have to learn when we're making advances—we have to not become arrogant, not become triumphal. We have to remember at all times, positive or negative, advances or setbacks, that even though we have the most profoundly scientific world outlook and methodology, we don't hold all the truth in our hands, and we never will.

So this is an important point that was emphasized in that series on anarchism, an important point we should recognize, not only before the seizure of power but after the seizure of power when we have a different responsibility as the vanguard of the proletariat and masses exercising state power and transforming society toward the eventual abolition of the state. We have to recognize there, too, that this is going to be true—that there are going to be people in different spheres of society or people who don't agree with the Party (or maybe are supporters but are not ready to make the leap to being communists fully) who have much of the truth "in their hands" or who are raising important questions that we need to be paying attention to.

If we're going to achieve our objectives in the most fundamental sense, if we're going to win in both senses—that is, if we're actually going to seize power and be able to carry out transformations *and* if we're going to do that guided by what our objectives are, to get to a whole different kind of world—winning in both those senses requires this kind of outlook and methodology, this kind of openness to the ideas, to the efforts, of others—and to their criticisms. Which doesn't mean we should tail people and doesn't mean we should agree with what we *don't* agree with. In other words, you can criticize me all day long, but if your criticism isn't valid to me, I'm not going to agree with it—and I shouldn't. Now, I may be wrong. Your criticism may be valid, but I'm like everybody else (everybody is this way, or should be): you have to be convinced. And it is true for everybody that, if you're not convinced, then eventually that's going to show up. You can be intimidated, or you can be overwhelmed, or you can be cajoled, but if you're not really won over, eventually the negative consequences of that are going to show up. So we shouldn't agree with people just because we want to be open. It's not a game we're playing; it's not a tactic; it's not a gimmick; it's not diplomacy. It's a question of fundamental methodology.

Struggling for the Truth

We should always struggle for what we understand to be true. We shouldn't be liberal and we shouldn't be relativist. Who knows, maybe tomorrow we'll discover that what we believe firmly today to be true is *not* true. That's true. [*B.A. laughs*] It is true that maybe tomorrow we'll discover that things we regard to be very foundational, as they say, are not completely true. But that doesn't mean we shouldn't put them forward as true now, if we understand them to be true now; because, if you don't do that, you disrupt the actual spiral or cycle of knowledge by which you learn more. You have to take those truths that you understand (or those things you understand to be true) at a given time and apply them—take them out into the world and put them into practice and see what they call forth, both in terms of what happens in reality and also in terms of what criticism is generated in relation to them—and then keep on learning, keep on carrying forward the practice-theory-practice dialectic. So we shouldn't be liberal and we shouldn't be relativist. We shouldn't agree with what we don't agree with just to get along with people, because that doesn't serve the very profound and world-historic objectives we have. We shouldn't tail people and we shouldn't concede to the idea, in our own thinking or in our dealings with other people, that there is no objective truth—it's only a few quirky MLMers who think there's objective reality or something. We're going to have to handle this contradiction correctly too.

Now, by way of negative example, to get at some of the points I'm trying to emphasize, we can look again at something that's pointed to in *GO&GS*[4]: the example of Lysenko, who was an agronomist, a scientist in the Soviet Union in the '30s, and whose ideas, profoundly incorrect ideas, were promoted by Stalin, even to the point of suppressing people who opposed his ideas. Without going into the whole thing here (it's been spoken to other places), basically Lysenko came up with theories that amounted to applying the principle of the inheritance of acquired characteristics, which is scientifically incorrect. They were in

---

4. *Great Objectives and Grand Strategy* is an unpublished work by Bob Avakian; excerpts from it have been published in *Revolutionary Worker* #1127-1142 (November 18, 2001 through March 10, 2002). They are available online at revcom.us.

a situation in the '30s where they needed to make some leaps in production overall—not just in general but also specifically staring in the face of what they could see was going to be a massive attack, or very likely a massive attack, from one of the most powerful military machines in the world at that time, namely German imperialism and its Nazi embodiment. They were very anxious, and Stalin was very concerned, to develop production. And here again things divide sharply into two in a number of ways, which are worth examining briefly.

On the one hand, it was necessary for them to prepare for that war. They could see from the early (or certainly from the mid) 1930s on—and especially from 1934 on, when the communist movement in Germany was decisively defeated and the Nazis were clearly consolidating power—that there was a very real and growing likelihood that they would be attacked by the Germans. And they had to prepare for that attack. So that was real. On the other hand—as may not surprise us, having looked into many of these things—Stalin had a lot of mechanical materialist tendencies with regard to this, too; and in a linear, one-to-one way, he equated, even expressly equated, production with being able to wage warfare (whoever can produce the most tanks, planes, etc., is going to win in modern warfare was pretty much the outlook that he was guided by). Now, they did produce a lot of tanks and planes, and they did ultimately win the warfare. Once again, short-term pragmatic logic might tell you: "Well, then, what's to criticize?" But there were problems in the way they went about this, which had longer-term consequences and ultimately strengthened the hand of the revisionists and in general the enemies of the Soviet revolution. So while it would be wrong, as an overall verdict, to say that their victory in World War 2 was a pyrrhic victory—a victory that really amounted to a defeat or that brought them to the threshold of defeat—it is, on the other hand, important to recognize that there were, in the way that they prepared for and carried out that war, significant aspects which were undermining the things that they were fighting for. And this is very important to learn from.

Now, I've always been very impatient with criticisms that are raised in a very facile manner about Stalin and "Stalinism" and the Soviet Union under Stalin's leadership without reckoning with the actual necessity that they were confronting. It's one thing to approach this, as we've tried to approach it, by seriously looking into all the complexity of what they were dealing with—the necessity they were confronted with, which was very profound and very stark—and then to wrestle with the question: how could they have done things better, and what can we learn by negative example as well as by positive example? But it's another thing to just sort of, in a very flippant way, dismiss that necessity—dismiss the fact that, for example, in Moscow, in the conditions of German invasion and occupation of a significant part of the country, for the better part of a year people were eating wallpaper, and the same in Leningrad, in order to hold out when they were under siege by the Germans. That's what they were reduced to. When you think about that, and you think of how Stalin saw that they were going to be confronted with tremendous necessity, it's another matter when you begin to discuss the errors that were made methodologically. They were made, and they were serious, but in order to correctly assess this, you have to situate it in the context of material, objective reality, of the actual necessity they were confronted with, and then look at how did they go about trying to deal with these contradictions, again sifting through what was correct and incorrect about this.

But, anyway, back to the Lysenko example. A number of scientists, including people who are sort of progressive scientists (not communists, but progressive scientists), have pointed out that to a large degree as a result of promoting Lysenko—and suppressing people who, more or less correctly from a scientific standpoint, opposed Lysenko's theories—biology (and in a larger sense, the sciences in general) in the Soviet Union suffered tremendously and science there has not really fully recovered, or is still confronting the question of recovering from the devastating effects of this—not just in a narrow and a pragmatic sense, but methodologically. So that's on the one hand. I think there's a lot of truth to that, and it's something very sobering to learn from. On the other hand, one of the things that has been pointed out is that a lot of the scientists who opposed Lysenko were counterrevolutionaries, or at least tended in that direction, politically and ideologically, and many of them had been the authorities in science, or at least in biology, in the Soviet Union up to that time. So here again is a sharp contradiction. But, in this Soviet experience and in the leadership of the Soviet Union, along with powerful pragmatic tendencies there was a certain assumption that since these people were counterrevolutionaries politically and ideologically, they must be wrong about this scientific question. Again, mechanical materialism, reductionism, not dealing correctly with the relation between the particular and the universal and between different levels of matter in motion, not understanding the discrete particularity of matter in motion while also correctly understanding the relation of the particular to the universal.

Striking Out in New Directions

And another dimension of this: I read an interesting article in the *New York Times* about an art exhibit in the U.S., I guess in New York itself. The headline of the article was "Change the World and Tweak the Bourgeoisie,"[5] and it was about this sort of avant-garde art in Russia in the period before and after the October Revolution and up till 1934. A lot of the art they described seems along the lines of surrealism, but these were expressly artists who were trying to, as they say, "tweak the bourgeoisie"—or trying to be subversive by being very outrageous in their art and sort of challenging every convention. I'm not very familiar with all the ins and outs of the art they talk about, but one thing that's interesting in the article that I did want to comment on is that, even after the October Revolution, a lot of these strains of art which we would not identify as being guided by a communist line were not suppressed and in fact in certain ways were continued and encouraged.

But then the article says that, after the death of Lenin in 1924, things began to change. The Communist Party called for an art "comprehensible to the millions." Well, let's take that statement. Is it important to have art that's comprehensible to the masses? Yes it is. Should art generally be incomprehensible to the masses? No. But here again you get into the complexities. We also don't want to feed the masses pablum in the artistic sphere, or anywhere else. In other words, it's correct—this was also argued for in those Ardea Skybreak articles in the *RW* on the social role of art[6]—it's correct to encourage the audience to struggle a bit in these spheres and not just to feed them pablum. You shouldn't deliberately make it impossible for them to comprehend what you're doing or create obstacles just for the sake of creating them, so to speak. But, on the other hand, people should be encouraged to struggle, and we shouldn't encourage philistinism among the masses—if something isn't immediately understandable, then it must not be any good. People should struggle for deeper meaning and to understand what people are doing with art, or in the sciences, etc. At the same time,

---

5. Holland Cotter, "Change the World and Tweak the Bourgeoisie," *New York Times* (March 29, 2002).

6. The four-part series by Ardea Skybreak, "Some Ideas on the Social Role of Art," appeared in *Revolutionary Worker* #1114-1117 (August 12-September 7, 2001).

we do need art that's more readily accessible to, more immediately comprehensible for, the millions. The question is, do we *only* need that? And the answer to that is no. Just as, in the scientific sphere, we don't only need things that have more immediate use or are more "technologically related," so in the sphere of art, while we do need art that's comprehensible to the millions, we don't only need that.

This is related to the principle that was discussed in *GO&GS* and was also incorporated into the Draft Programme as follows: "Our proletarian ideology leads us to appreciate the importance of science and other intellectual and artistic work that more directly serves the ongoing struggle of the proletariat, on the one hand; and, on the other hand, to appreciate scientific inquiry and intellectual engagement and artistic expression which is not tied in such a direct way—and certainly not in a pragmatic, 'instrumentalist' way—to the policy and more immediate aims of the proletarian party at any given time." I think this applies to the questions: do we need art that is comprehensible to the masses, on the one hand, and should we allow for some abstract art and art that's not so immediately comprehensible, on the other hand?

The *New York Times* article goes on to say that, in the mid-'30s—or, interestingly, 1934 in particular, which is where the art in this exhibit ends—"Stalin decreed that socialist realist painting was the only acceptable aesthetic style." We know that there are a lot of problems associated with only "socialist realism." This is why Mao spoke about needing to combine revolutionary realism with revolutionary romanticism. It's also why this is in that statement in *For a Harvest of Dragons*[7] where it talks about how we need our firmness of principle, but also flexibility...we need realism, but also romanticism. We need it in the sphere of art, but we need it everywhere; we need people to be using their imagination and striking out in new directions, even in terms of political questions, in terms of solving problems in any sphere, or even just investigating them without an eye to an immediate solution. We need that, even while we also need things that do more immediately relate to our objectives and things that are more immediately comprehensible to the masses.

So this is another way in which we have to correctly handle contradictions. This not only relates to our more immediate objectives—not only to winning in the sense of advancing the class struggle and get-

---

7. Avakian, *For a Harvest of Dragons: On the "Crisis of Marxism" and the Power of Marxism—Now More Than Ever* (Chicago: RCP Publications, 1983), p. 152.

ting over the hump of seizing power and beginning to carry out the socialist transformation—but it applies in the largest sense. This has to do with what we're all about. We are not about a narrow and pragmatic way of approaching reality—and certainly not an instrumentalist way, which in essence means that, in place of what should be the search for the truth, you undertake a process of seeking desired ends, you pervert the process that should be the search for the truth into an attempt to tautologically verify assumptions that you've already drawn *a priori*: you make an assumption and set out to prove it, rather than to really engage reality. We don't want that in terms of developing the struggle, and we don't want it in the broadest sense of what we're all about. The kind of world we're trying to bring into being is not a world which is guided by instrumentalist and narrow and pragmatic thinking, or the notion that only that which is already accepted can be done. Lenin criticized revisionism politically for saying—or he pointed out that revisionism amounts to saying—that what is desirable is whatever's possible, and what's possible is what is already being done. That's not a "recipe"—not that we really want recipes, but that's not a method—for making revolution, and it's also not an outlook and methodology that's going to lead to or is in accord with everything we're setting out to do, with what our ultimate and highest objectives are.

THERE IS NO RELIGIOUS BASIS, THERE IS A POWERFUL, MATERIAL BASIS, FOR COMMUNISM [1]

Stepping back and looking at things with historical sweep, and harking back to what was said earlier, in the part of this talk on philosophical and methodological questions—on applying materialism and dialectics to confront and transform reality as it actually is, as it is moving and changing and as it is actually tending in its motion and development—this is the basis for Lenin's statement (which was referred to in *Great Objectives and Grand Strategy*[2]) on dreaming, and on bringing our dreams into reality. It is the basis for the point from Mao (also referred to in *GO&GS*) on striving for greatness, not for ourselves or for some personal gain, but for our class and our cause. It is the basis, in other words, for our "strategic double-c": strategic contempt for our enemy and its system, and strategic confidence in our class and our cause. With all the complexity of social reality and its historical development; and, more broadly, with all the complexity of reality and its motion and development; with all that, our historic goal of world communism is not just "a good idea." It is emphatically that, but it's *not just* that. It is in fact the way the world is tending.

Here it's important to emphasize what was said in the *Democracy*

---

1. This selection is from the talk *Grasp Revolution, Promote Production: Questions of Outlook and Method, Some Points on the New Situation,* excerpts from which appeared in *Revolutionary Worker* from November 2002 through March 2003 and are available online at revcom.us. This particular selection was published in *Revolutionary Worker* #1189 (March 2, 2003).

2. *Great Objectives and Grand Strategy (GO&GS)* is an unpublished work by Bob Avakian. Excerpts from it have appeared in the *Revolutionary Worker* #1127-1142 (November 18, 2001 through March 10, 2002). These excerpts are available online at revcom.us.

book:[3] that we cannot say that communism is inevitable in some meta-physical and idealist or essentially religious sense—in the sense that there is some predetermined, predestined way in which all of reality and all of human historical development in particular has been leading up to, or even was somehow *bound* to lead up to, communism. (This is also spoken to in GO&GS and it is something we've given emphasis to repeatedly.) We cannot say that. And this has to do with something I wrote, which was cited at the beginning of the book *Of Primeval Steps and Future Leaps* by Ardea Skybreak, about how it's wrong to say that the emergence of the human species or the development of human society was somehow predetermined or that there are some predetermined or predestined pathways that reality in general or human historical development in particular was bound to follow.

At the same time, harking back to something I stressed earlier in this talk, this is not all random or accident.[4] While we can't look at it as predetermined and predestined in some religious sense, there is the continuing dialectic between accident and necessity, there's the ongoing fact that what's accident in one context is necessity in another (and vice versa); and there are certain underlying causes and forces that have been at play through all this, though nothing was predetermined or bound to turn out the way it has turned out. We must willingly and decisively let go of and gladly reject all such essentially religious notions, and we need to uproot the religious mentality from within the communist movement as well as within society as a whole, ultimately—but especially right now we need to struggle against these tendencies in our own ranks.

At the same time, all of human history, in all its diversity and complexity, has *in fact* led humanity to the threshold of communism—has established a powerful material and social basis for this, not just in this or that country, but throughout the world, notwithstanding the differentiated and highly contradictory character of the world situation and of world conditions. This is a leap that humanity needs to make and in historical terms is now poised to make. And there is, as I said,

---

3. Bob Avakian, *Democracy: Can't We Do Better Than That?* (Chicago: Banner Press, 1986).

4. The relation between accident and necessity, or contingency and cause, is discussed in the first excerpt from the talk *Grasp Revolution, Promote Production: Questions of Outlook and Method, Some Points on the New Situation*, "The New Situation, The Need for Dynamic Resistance," in *Revolutionary Worker* No. 1143 (November 17, 2002). Available online at revcom.us.

the dialectical relation running through all this, between accident and necessity, between contingency and underlying driving forces which set the basic framework for things.

Now, to paraphrase an important point from Marx, people make history, but they don't make it simply according to their will or their imagination; they make it in accordance with, and by transforming, the conditions that confront them at any given time. This is an extremely important point. And, yet once more [*B.A. laughs*], this is a unity of opposites: people make history, on the one hand; but, on the other hand, they don't make it simply according to their will or their imagination or desires, that is, on a voluntarist basis. They make it in accordance with and by transforming objective material reality, the necessity or the conditions that confront them at a given time. Fully exploring the implications of that is something that's very important and worthwhile doing in an ongoing way.

Of course, as we are coming to understand more and more deeply and fully, making the world-historical leap to communism will be, is bound to be, a complex and a wrenching process, one full of twists and turns—and, as we have said before, full of great leaps forward and inevitably great setbacks and reversals, to be followed by yet further great leaps forward. All this is rooted in the fact that the actual development of human society, in all its diversity and complexity, over thousands of years and throughout the world, has led to the emergence of the capitalist system and the bourgeois epoch and the increasing development of this system, particularly in its highest and final stage of imperialism, as a *worldwide* system (even though, as I've been emphasizing here and as we've spoken to in *America in Decline* and "Notes on Political Economy,"[5] this is not a uniform and undifferentiated system throughout the world, but consists in and proceeds through profound divisions, including the great divide between the imperialist states and the oppressed nations and countries of the world, as well as the divisions and conflicts among the imperialist states themselves).

Through all this, the fundamental contradiction of the capitalist system, between socialized production and private appropriation—and the motion and major contradictions that this fundamental contradiction gives rise to and repeatedly intensifies, through a spiral-like devel-

---

5. Raymond Lotta with Frank Shannon, *America in Decline* (Chicago: Banner Press, 1984); "Notes on Political Economy" by the Revolutionary Communist Party, USA (Chicago: RCP Publications, 2000).

opment, on a worldwide basis—all this continues to assert itself and to call forth its opposite: resistance, struggle, revolution, and—at the core of this, able to act as a driving force within all of this—the potential gravedigger of this system, the proletariat. This remains profoundly true, even more profoundly true than at the time Marx proclaimed it, despite the attempts of the bourgeoisie to mock it and to pretend that there is no proletariat, and certainly no more prospect of proletarian revolution. Well, we shall see. And this will continue to assert itself through all the setbacks as well as the advances of our world-historic struggle: the need for proletarian revolution and the fact that there is no other ultimate resolution to the fundamental contradiction of capitalism and the bourgeois epoch—no other resolution which holds out and represents a future for humanity, no other resolution that is in the interests of the great majority of the world's people and ultimately of humanity as a whole.

Now, once again, we have to face reality squarely, whether it's unpleasant or not. Could some other outcome, something different than the ultimate triumph of the world proletarian revolution and the future of communism, result from all this—from the motion and conflict that arises from this fundamental contradiction? Could all the volcanic eruption and the antagonistic contention that is called forth out of all this lead to a yet more horrendous result, even perhaps the destruction of humanity? Well, yes, as we have said before, this is possible, and we have to face the fact that there is no certainty or guarantee of the triumph of the world proletarian revolution in some basically religious sense.

Once again, we have to let go of and reject all such notions, and do so gladly and willingly. But, while such a profoundly negative outcome cannot be declared impossible, it certainly can be said that *it* is far from inevitable. And it must be emphasized that the fact that the ultimate outcome is not predetermined or predestined means precisely that it can be and will be determined by the struggle among people, and fundamentally social classes and their conscious representatives and leaderships. So in this we can see that there is a tremendous scope for the initiative of the proletarian vanguard forces and tremendous importance to what we do. The recognition of all this should not lead to fatalism and pessimism; rather, it should lead us to a heightened understanding of the tremendously important role of our conscious initiative and of the conscious initiative of the masses that we must work to increasingly unleash. In this world-historic struggle, while there are great difficulties and powerful forces that we will have to confront and defeat, there are also profoundly powerful material and social forces that are strategically favorable for our side, for our cause.

Another Look at the "History of the 20th Century"

Applying these principles in response to all the talk about "the history of the 20th century" is extremely important. The "history of the 20th century" has become shorthand for all the alleged horrors of the attempts at communist revolution, or of socialist society in the Soviet Union and in China. I was watching a videotape of when Boots from the Coup was on the TV talk show *Politically Incorrect*, and at one point he came out and said very boldly, "Well, I'm a communist," and there was all this sort of rumble and rustling. Then the host of the show, Bill Maher, says: "Haven't you heard about the history of the 20th century?" By which he actually meant: "Haven't you gotten the memo?" This is important for us to confront and refute.

The history of the 20th century is not the history of the debacle and disaster and the horrendous nature of the attempts at proletarian revolution against the will of the people and against the current of reality, or whatever. In fact, it's a contradictory history, but what stands out very sharply, when it's understood in its real terms, are the tremendous achievements of our class, particularly where it has seized and held power and carried out transformations of society in every sphere. And it can be stated without any hesitation or any equivocation, or any sense of being successfully refuted, that if you take the experience of the masses of people in the Soviet Union during the period when it was actually socialist—with all the difficulties, and with all the errors, even grievous errors, that were made by the leadership, in particular Stalin—and if you take the experience of the Chinese masses during the period when China was socialist, there's absolutely no question that, by any measure and with regard to every sphere of society, the masses were *qualitatively* and *infinitely* better off than they were before or have been since. This is something we have to boldly grasp and put forward and struggle for, against "the memo" on "the history of the 20th century."

Back in the early '70s we used to send delegations to China—not only Party delegations but also delegations of people from different sections of society (students, workers, and so on). And I remember, after one workers' delegation, we had a dinner for one of the people who went on the delegation, and we invited some other people over—some other people we were working with, proletarians. And they were asking this person who'd gone on the delegation, "Well, what was it like going to China?" And he answered, "Oh, it was like stepping through a time machine." And this other person, who wasn't particularly backward but was thinking in terms of the usual portrayal about the backwardness of the conditions in China, said, "Kind of like going into the past, huh?" And the person who'd been to China replied: "No! The future!" This wasn't a case of people who were taken to something like the famous (or infamous) Potemkin Village in Tsarist Russia, where they set up a phony facade to make the society seem more advanced and "ideal" than it was. This was reflecting the reality of what they'd seen and learned about in China.

And this is something we have to grasp very firmly and deeply and stand on boldly—and also propagate and struggle for among people, to sum up correctly the history of the 20th century and the real debacle and horrors of the imperialist system and, on the other side, the tremendous achievements of our class in the socialist states that we brought into being. Even though those beginning efforts have been reversed, and there is a tremendous amount we have to sum up more and more deeply from that—and not shrink from recognizing all the negative aspects and learning from all the errors—we have to very boldly and forthrightly put forward the truth. Not just something we'd *like* to be true, but the actual truth about the tremendous achievements of our class and its socialist states so far, and the fact that this represents only the beginning stages, which we have to learn to build on and to leap beyond.

So, reflecting on and grappling with all this, we can see perhaps even more deeply how the conclusion from Mao stands out in the profound way in which, in pointing to all the complexity and, yes, all the difficulty, it concentrates the essence of this world-historic process and struggle: the future is bright, the road is tortuous.

MARXISM AND THE ENLIGHTENMENT [1]

Particularly with questions in mind that relate to the arts, sciences and the intellectual realm in general, I recently read a book called *Science, Jews, and Secular Culture* (which is a collection of essays and lectures by David A. Hollinger).[2] Although it approaches things from a different viewpoint than ours, this book does speak to many of the important questions concerning intellectuals and their role in relation to the larger society and societal objectives with which I have been wrestling for some time, including in various writings and talks (for example, in some of the essays in *Reflections, Sketches, & Provocations*,[3] then in "End/Beginning,"[4] and in more recent talks and writings). Hollinger does provide some important historical background and some insights into the key questions at issue, which of course we have to sift through and synthesize as part of applying our outlook and methodology.

Discussing various intellectual currents and influences from the 1920s to the present—with particular attention to the post WW2 period and focusing especially on academia and more specifically on the struggle of Jews to break down barriers there and, in turn, their overall

---

1. This selection is from *Great Objectives and Grand Strategy*, a talk given by Bob Avakian at the end of the 1990s. Excerpts from it have been published in the *Revolutionary Worker* #1127-1142 (November 18, 2001 through March 10, 2002) and are available online at revcom.us. This particular selection was published in *Revolutionary Worker* #1129 (December 2, 2001).

2. David A. Hollinger, *Science, Jews, and Secular Culture: Studies in Mid-Twentieth-Century American Intellectual History* (Princeton, N.J.: Princeton University Press, 1996).

3. *Reflections, Sketches and Provocations* (Chicago: RCP Publications, 1990).

4. Avakian, "The End of a Stage—The Beginning of a New Stage," *Revolution*, Issue 60 (Fall 1990).

positive influence on academia and more generally on intellectual thought in America—Hollinger touches on the question of "intellectual inquiry" *per se*—or "in its own right"—vs. social and political influences and "agendas." He traces how, during WW2, a major strain in American academic and intellectual circles was to wage an intellectual and more broadly a cultural struggle (a *Kulturkampf*) against the Nazis and their ideology, and how later, during the early years of the "Cold War" in particular, a similar "Kulturkampf" (or cultural war) was directed against the Soviet Union (and "Stalinism").

In a chapter entitled "Free Enterprise and Free Inquiry: The Emergence of Laissez-Faire Communitarianism in the Ideology of Science in the United States," Hollinger shows how a significant tendency within intellectual circles, in the U.S. in particular, has been (as the chapter title suggests) the notion of *laissez-faire* individualism as the ethos of science and the best means for its progress—the linking of "free inquiry" with the "free market." For example, he discusses theories prominent in the 1920s and '30s which "shared the assumption that knowledge was something autonomous, an entity that could be trusted to shape society since its own shape was produced by truths external to, and somehow above, society. In this view, science was to be left alone just as the market was to be left alone in classical political economy." (p. 103) Yet, especially with the growth of "support" for science by the bourgeois state and bourgeois "private foundations," through and after WW2, there was an increased recognition that there were limits to this "laissez-faire individualism": "But massive federal funding and the creation of an attendant bureaucracy eventually forced the recognition that someone was going to have to decide exactly who would get the money and why." (p. 108) Someone is going to have to decide—that's a very important point. (In fact this is a point that I emphasized—and whose implications I explored—particularly in relation to socialist society, in the "open letters" to Stephen Jay Gould, Carl Sagan, and Isaac Asimov that are in a collection of essays I wrote some years ago, *Reflections, Sketches, & Provocations*.)

Hollinger's discussion touches on how various intellectuals have perceived the mission of Western civilization—or the "modernizing" and "civilizing" mission of Western intellectual thought and culture, especially as embodied in science. He writes:

> "We also see these intellectuals offering science to the
> rest of the world in much the same perspective from which

their loquacious ally [British scientist and novelist C.P.] Snow was calling for the spread of the scientific spirit to Africa and Asia. *The Dynamics of Modernization*, by the Princeton historian Cyril Black, identified 'the scientific attitude' as the most important single motor of the entire modernization process from early modern Europe to the present. Industry, technology, and democracy followed eventually in the wake of this distinctive mentality.

"The modernizing process was generally understood to entail the making of the entire world over according to the model of what the United States had become by the early and mid-1960s." (p.167)

This relates to questions bound up with the Enlightenment and how we have to, from our perspective, divide the Enlightenment in two. In previous talks, I spoke to what Marxism holds in common with the general thinking associated with the Enlightenment, and what we disagree with and have to make a radical rupture with. This is very important these days, and also very complex, because there are various strains of imperialist and reactionary thought relating to the Enlightenment. There is a certain kind of all-out assault on the Enlightenment, from religious fundamentalists and obscurantists, including the "Religious Right" in the U.S., who identify the Enlightenment—and in particular the concept of reliance on science and rationality, rather than obscurantist religious notions, as the foundation for ideology and politics—as the dawning of the age of the devil, so to speak. On the other hand, as indicated by some of the intellectual trends Hollinger examines, there is a definite strain in bourgeois liberal thinking to conceive of the Enlightenment (and what are considered its results) as a "positive" instrument of colonialism and of an imperialist domination that seeks to remake the whole world in the image of bourgeois democracy.

The point I want to focus on here, with regard to the Enlightenment and the continuing contention around its influence, is that Marxism agrees with that aspect of the Enlightenment that says that the world is knowable, that people should seek to understand the world (or reality generally) in all its complexity, and that they should do so by scientific methods. Now, there is a difference, a profound difference, between bourgeois scientific methods and the scientific method of dialectical and historical materialism, but it is a tenet and a basic premise of the Enlightenment that people should seek to understand the world by scientific methods, and this is a principal reason why the Enlightenment has been brought under attack—and today is once again being brought under attack—by religious obscurantists and other reactionary trends. That's the aspect of the Enlightenment with which, in a general sense, Marxism agrees.

What it disagrees with is, first of all, the notion that (to invoke a certain irony by quoting the Christian Bible) "you shall know the truth and the truth shall set you free." This is not true, in the final analysis. First of all, what's in the Bible is not the truth. But even if it were, just knowing what the truth is and thinking that in itself will "set you free" is a form of rationalism (of idealism); it goes along with this idea that science will re-make the world by mere force of its "truths." It is the same basic outlook that I criticize in the open letter to Gould (and others) speaking to his statement that eventually the Catholic Church relented on its difference with Galileo because, after all, Galileo's views of the solar system were much more correct than the Church's, and the Church had to accede to that reality. I pointed out that there is some validity to Gould's argument, but that there are also many, many profound truths that the Catholic Church and other religious institutions and authorities still do not acknowledge—not the least of which is that God does not exist! So, it's not just a matter of what is true; there is also the fact that social struggle—and, in class society, class struggle—has to take place in order for ideas, even ones that represent profound truths, to become "operative" in society, to be taken up and applied by society as a whole. And this gets back to Marx's insistence that the point is not merely to understand the world, but to change it.

So that's an important way, philosophically, in which Marxism differs from the core thought of the Enlightenment, or the rationalism that's integral to the Enlightenment. And, at the same time, of course, politically, the revolutionary proletariat opposes and represents a radical rupture with the system of bourgeois political rule which essentially corresponds to the Enlightenment. And, more particularly, we oppose the use of the Enlightenment, and the scientific and technological advances associated with it, as a way of effecting and justifying colonialism and imperialist domination, in the name of "the white man's burden" or the alleged "civilizing mission" of the "more enlightened and advanced" imperialist system, and so on. This is another way in which we differ, profoundly, from at least important aspects of how the Enlightenment (and associated things) have been applied.

Returning to what Hollinger has to say on important aspects of this—significantly (and this relates to some points I have emphasized in discussing the role of religion in American society in this period), Hollinger writes that:

> "The 'conflict between science and religion' is a set phrase that historians of the United States associate the most directly with the second half of the nineteenth century, and for good reasons. It was in the wake of the Darwinian revolution in natural history that American Protestants displayed their most acute anxiety about the relation of scientific innovation to inherited Christian doctrine. This anxiety, which was often expressed through the argument that the very idea of a 'conflict' between science and religion was based on a misunderstanding of the issues [and here I would interject that we hear this very same argument today; but in any case, this anxiety, says Hollinger], had long since diminished by the middle decades of the twentieth century. But in the milder culture wars of the era of World War II and immediately following, one can hear several echoes of these earlier spiritual disputes." (p. 155)

(As an aside here—and this would seem to relate to why Pope John Paul II decided not to join the Protestant fundamentalist reactionaries in attacking evolution, but instead chose to declare evolution compatible with religious belief—it is worth noting that Hollinger writes a little later: "In the meantime, the relationship of Catholic commitment to American intellectual and political life had been transformed by the replacement of Spanish and Italian fascism with the 'Godless' Communist menace of the Cold War, by the political success of President John Kennedy, by the liberalization of Vatican II, and by the influence of John Courtney Murray. The tension between the secular intelligentsia and Catholicism was dramatically diminished; Catholics were no longer assumed to be enemies of liberal intellectuals."—p.167)

Hollinger also shows how certain "conservative" intellectuals have made use of intellectual tendencies and debates—including, interestingly, those generally involving "post-modernism"—to try to undermine science and promote fundamentalist religious obscurantism and in particular the fundamentalist Christian view of the world and theory of knowledge (to make "an orthodox version of the biblical episteme" the legitimate means of acquiring an understanding of things):

"I invoke post-modernism to remind us of the familiar story of Kuhn's appropriation and use by intellectuals of the 1970s and 1980s who depicted science as an authoritarian, 'totalizing' project that impedes rather than promotes truly democratic and egalitarian values....

"The representation of science in post-modernist discourse is so close to us today that I need do no more in this lecture than allude to it. Yet there is one element in the contemporary scene to which I want to call attention in closing. This is the recent, increasingly assertive claim of conservative Christians that Kuhn and Foucault and their followers have disproven the objectivity of science and thus have rendered an orthodox version of the biblical episteme cognitively legitimate once again." (p. 171)

All this emphasizes yet again that what is required is the synthesis that only the consistent application of our ideology, MLM, can provide. And all this underscores, as well, the importance of our basic understanding that, on the one hand, truth does not have a class character while, on the other hand, the means for arriving at the truth in the fullest sense—and for acting, in the most systematic and comprehensive way, to change the world in accordance with reality and its motion and development—is represented by the outlook and methodology of one class in this era, the proletariat.

At the same time, precisely this proletarian world outlook and methodology should lead us to handle the contradictions with intellectuals, as well as artists (and generally the sphere of ideology, including culture) in a dialectical and not a crude, mechanical and narrow way. It should lead us *both* to appreciate the importance of science and other intellectual (and artistic) work that *does* more directly serve the ongoing struggle of the proletariat, and the importance of a fundamentally collective framework and approach to intellectual (and artistic) work, on the one hand; *and* on the *other* hand, to appreciate scientific inquiry and intellectual engagement (and artistic experimentation as well) which is not tied in such a direct way—and certainly not in a pragmatic, "instrumentalist" way—to the policy and more immediate aims of the proletarian party (and the proletarian state where that exists) at any given time, and which allows for and encourages the initiative of individuals, within the overall collective framework and spirit.

The many different aspects of this should be approached in such a way that it all contributes, in an overall and ultimate sense, to the larger revolutionary cause of the proletariat. As should be obvious, and as I have emphasized a number of times, these are not easy contradictions to handle correctly—but this is a challenge we must meet if we are going to make the world-historic advance to communism and achieve those two radical ruptures, with traditional property relations and traditional ideas.

ABOUT BOB AVAKIAN

Bob Avakian is Chairman of the Revolutionary Communist Party, USA. A veteran of the Free Speech Movement and the revolutionary upsurges of the 1960s and early 1970s, he worked closely with the Black Panther Party. By the mid-1970s, he emerged as the foremost Maoist revolutionary in the United States. He has guided the RCP since its formation in 1975 and is a major leader of the international communist movement. Over the last twenty-five years, Avakian has produced a highly significant body of work, and he approaches Marxism as a living, developing science that must be constantly interrogating itself.

Avakian has penned the most comprehensive account of Mao's theoretical contributions to Marxism. He has been undertaking an ongoing examination of the experience of proletarian revolution in the twentieth century—its great achievements, in particular the profound lessons of the Cultural Revolution in China, as well as its setbacks, shortcomings, and mistakes. He has been addressing issues of revolutionary strategy in the U.S. and for the international movement. He has analyzed why revolution is not only necessary but also possible within the U.S. itself.

Through these and other critical investigations, Avakian has been bringing forward a vision of socialism and communism that breaks vital new ground for Marxism and the communist project. He has been deepening and enlarging the understanding of the tasks and contradictions bound up with the exercise of revolutionary authority and how the masses can be unleashed to rule and transform society. In recent writings, he has been speaking to the indispensable role of dissent in socialist society—how it contributes to deeper knowledge of socialist society, the critical spirit that must permeate it, and the continuing struggle to transform socialist society towards communism. He has been drawing attention to the importance of the intellectual and cultural spheres in socialist society and in the revolutionary process overall, and he probes historic problems in the understanding and approach of the international communist movement. In works such as *Conquer the World?—The International Proletariat Must and Will* and *Getting Over the Two Great Humps: Further Thoughts on Conquering the World*, he has been conceptualizing the international dimensions of communist revolution in ways that have far-reaching implications for the world struggle.

Avakian's writings are marked by great breadth—from discussions about religion and atheism and morality, to the limits of classical democracy, to basketball. It is often alleged that a vanguard party is incompatible with a searching, critical, and creative intellectual enterprise. Avakian gives the lie to this claim.

From his life experience and revolutionary perspective comes a profound sense of the struggles and sentiments among the masses of people; and he keeps his finger on the pulse of the movements of opposition in society more broadly. This is a revolutionary leader who has said about leadership: "if you don't have a poetic spirit—or at least a poetic side—it is very dangerous for you to lead a Marxist movement or be the leader of a socialist state."

Bob Avakian is the visionary leader of a Maoist vanguard party, the Revolutionary Communist Party, which has its sights on the revolutionary seizure of power and the radical transformation of society in the colossus that is late imperial America—all as part of a worldwide process of revolutionary struggle whose final aim is communism, a world without exploitative and oppressive relations and the corresponding political structures, institutions, and ideas and culture.

* * * * *

The author and Insight Press welcome readers' comments about this book. Correspondence should be addressed c/o Insight Press, 4064 N. Lincoln Ave. #264, Chicago, IL 60618. Additional information about the author can be found at www.insight-press.com.

Several other websites contain further information and works by the author:

• **bobavakian.net**—contains various resources, including downloadable audio recordings of recent talks by and question-and-answer sessions with Bob Avakian.

• **revcom.us**—the official website of *Revolution* newspaper, voice of the Revolutionary Communist Party, USA; includes an extensive collection of articles and other material written by Bob Avakian. *Revolution* regularly publishes articles by Bob Avakian, and is published weekly in English and Spanish editions. For subscription information, write to Revolution, Box 3486, Merchandise Mart, Chicago, IL 60654.

• **threeQvideo.com**—website of Three Q Productions, producer of the video *Revolution: Why It's Necessary, Why It's Possible, What It's All About*, a film of a 2003 talk by Bob Avakian. The video, in DVD or VHS format, can be ordered online.

Also by Bob Avakian

*The Loss in China and the Revolutionary Legacy
of Mao Tsetung*

Mao Tsetung's Immortal Contributions

Conquer the World? The International Proletariat Must and Will

*For a Harvest of Dragons: On the "Crisis of Marxism" and the Power
of Marxism, Now More Than Ever*

A Horrible End, or an End to the Horror?

*Bullets from the Writings, Speeches, and Interviews
of Bob Avakian, Chairman of the
Revolutionary Communist Party, USA*

Democracy: Can't We Do Better Than That?

Reflections, Sketches & Provocations

The End of a Stage – The Beginning of a New Stage

Radical Ruptures, or Yes, Mao More Than Ever

*In the Aftermath of the Persian Gulf War, More on
Could We Really Win?: Prospects for Revolution*

*Preaching from a Pulpit of Bones: We Need Morality But Not
Traditional Morality*

*On War and Revolution, On Being a Revolutionary and Changing the
World* (audio interview with Carl Dix)

*Grasp Revolution, Promote Production – Questions of Outlook and
Method, Some Points on the New Situation*

Reaching for the Heights and Flying Without a Safety Net

*Revolution: Why It's Necessary, Why It's Possible,
What It's All About* (video/DVD)

*Dictatorship and Democracy, and the Socialist Transition to
Communism*

*Phony Communism is Dead . . . Long Live Real Communism!
(Second Edition with Appendix Democracy: More Than Ever,
We Can and Must Do Better Than That)*

*From Ike to Mao . . . and Beyond, My Journey from Mainstream
America to Revolutionary Communist, a Memoir by Bob Avakian*

*Marxism and the Call of the Future: Conversations on Ethics, History,
and Politics* (with Bill Martin)